INSCAPE 2018

Washburn University
Department of English
1700 SW College Ave
Topeka, KS 66621

I hope to stand with those who love
their lives in time to live them,
bravely, between kisses, under stars.

—Robin Becker

Vol. 43

inscapemagazine.org
washburn.edu/inscape
facebook.com/inscapemagazine

Cover Art: Detail from *Up, Up, and Away,* by Michael Young
acrylic, 28x34

Inscape, published by the English Department at Washburn University in Topeka, Kansas, features poetry, fiction, nonfiction, and visual art from the region and beyond.

INSCAPE 2018

FICTION

NONFICTION

POETRY

ART

Root Revealed
Justin Marable
serigraph/monoprint
16x17

EDITORS' CHOICE

Fossil Fuel
Justin Marable
serigraph/monoprint
30x22

The Candidate

Jim O'Loughlin

When we're hiring a new professor, we all have an ideal candidate in mind. We want to hire a visionary, a future Nobel laureate, a colleague who will redefine Science and inspire all of us, fellow scientists and students alike, to rededicate ourselves to the pursuit of truth and understanding.

This story isn't about that. No, it's about the worst job candidate we ever had. I bear some responsibility here. I was chairing the search committee and had agreed to bring him in for an on-campus interview, even though I had my doubts. While his written materials were fine, when we did a phone interview, something about him seemed a bit off. There were a lot of long pauses, and we couldn't tell if that was because of the candidate or due to a poor phone connection. But one of the other committee members, whom I will only identify as "the grumpy professor," was sure he was the only candidate worth our consideration.

So we brought him into town, and I immediately saw that something was wrong. When I met him at the airport, I wasn't sure at first that he was the candidate. He was oddly underdressed, in a flannel shirt and torn jeans, and he needed a shave, but what was really weird was that he wouldn't make eye contact with me. When I welcomed him and assured him that our current cold weather was unusual (only a slight fib), he stared down at his shoes. On the drive from the airport, he stared out the window and only responded in monosyllables. I found myself talking a lot, about the university's new science center and about our students, discussing the local housing market, the K–12 school system. By the time we reached the hotel, I had burned through most of my material.

At least he brightened up when we got to the hotel. At check in, we had a small gift basket waiting for him. He immediately grabbed an apple from it and began chomping into it while the desk clerk ran through the hotel amenities. I saw the first sign of emotion from him when he was told that the hotel had a pool he could use. "Is it indoors?" he asked.

The clerk, reasonably enough, looked at him like he was crazy. There was a foot of snow on the ground and more in the forecast. It has been at least three weeks since temperatures had been above freezing. Yes, she said, the pool was indoors.

It was an odd beginning, but I told myself not to make too much of it. The candidate was likely nervous. God knows I had been when I was first on the job market and was the first female scientist hired by our department. I left him my phone number, told him that someone from the committee would meet him for breakfast, and said good night. On the drive home, I got a call. It was the candidate, asking if we would pay for any movies he rented through the hotel's system. I paused. I wasn't sure how to answer, but I said I thought it would be reasonable for us to pick up the tab for a movie. "Just one?" he asked. "Yes," I said, more definitively. "Just one."

It got worse. The next morning, one of the committee members—in fact, the grumpy professor, who had insisted that we bring this candidate in for an interview—was to meet him for breakfast, and then bring him over to campus. That morning I was in my office going through email, when there was a sharp rap on the door and the grumpy professor burst in. His face was ashen.

"I am so sorry," he said to me, his hands shaking.

"What? Did something happen?" I replied.

"The candidate..."

"What? Did something happen to him?"

"Well, I suppose something did. Probably a traumatic childhood."

"No, I mean did something happen to him at breakfast?"

"There is something seriously wrong with him. We need to cancel the interview."

"Slow down. We can't cancel the interview. What happened at breakfast?"

The grumpy professor then launched into a description of a truly bizarre meal in which the candidate ordered three different breakfasts and then refused to talk, saying he was saving himself for the interview.

"I had to sit there and watch him eat. For over an hour! And he chewed with his mouth open the whole time!"

None of this was good, but of course being eccentric didn't disqualify someone from being hired as a professor. In fact, eccentricity might have been the only thing our department members all had in common. I told the grumpy professor to please give this candidate the benefit of the doubt, since we hadn't even officially started the interview.

Well, you won't be surprised that the interview was a disaster. The candidate still refused to make eye contact, still responded to questions in monosyllables, and then—and this one is still unbelievable to me—stopped in the middle of the interview to respond to a text message. Fortunately, the candidate was next slated for a campus tour with one of our undergraduates, because our committee was in shock.

"I think we should just cancel his research presentation and put an end to this," the grumpy professor insisted once the candidate had left.

I said we had an obligation, ethically and probably legally, to give this candidate the same consideration as anyone else we brought to campus. We couldn't treat him differently just because he had performed poorly so far.

Then I got a call. It was the student who was giving the candidate his campus tour. She seemed nervous. She said the candidate had told her that he wanted to check out the neighborhood immediately off campus and that he would get lunch on his own and find his way back later.

I audibly sighed. Things continued going wrong. The candidate was late getting back for his meeting with the dean, who had perhaps the tightest schedule on campus, and who gave me an annoyed and perplexed look when I came by afterwards to pick the candidate up. The candidate's formal research presentation was poorly attended, which was perhaps a blessing in disguise, since it consisted of him reading sections of his dissertation's literature review word-for-word off of PowerPoint slides. When our youngest junior professor, a very sweet, very tiny woman with a soft voice, asked him to "clarify a point from the presentation," he practically bit her head off, shouting, "Did you not hear what I said?"

The exit interview with the committee was brief. We all just wanted it to be over. Afterward, the junior professor came to me and said she couldn't drive him to his hotel because she wouldn't feel safe alone in a car with him. The grumpy professor told me he refused to have another meal with the candidate.

That left me, as the committee chair, having to deal with him. I recommended an early dinner at a restaurant on the same block as his hotel. The candidate shrugged. We had a quiet drive to the restaurant, and he got us a table while I called my husband to explain why I wouldn't be home. When I got to the table, the candidate already had an open bottle of wine and an appetizer plate of oysters in front of him.

I sat down, not expecting him to look up at me. I wasn't disappointed. Nor had the grumpy professor been exaggerating about the candidate's table manners. I may never be able to eat oysters again. When it came time to order I had to stop him before he asked for multiple entrees. "I'm sorry," I said. "The university can only pay for one entree."

The candidate shrugged and order the lobster/steak combo, which was the most expensive item on the menu. I had a salad. I tried to get the candidate to talk about the day and how he felt things had gone. He shrugged. He ate. I talked about the university. He did not seem interested. I started to get a headache. When he tried to order another bottle of wine, I said no, the dinner was over. I'm sure my voice had a tone, but the candidate just shrugged again. I paid the bill and we left.

The weather had turned. Snow had begun falling while we had been eating, and it covered the ground like a white sheet, muffling the sounds of traffic.

"Well, I don't remember that being in the forecast," I said.

The candidate said nothing, and I had had it.

“Look,” I said, “when someone makes an innocuous comment about the weather, you are supposed to make a similar, inconsequential response. It’s how people relate to each other. If you can’t make that minimal gesture, I’m not sure you are suited for interaction with humans.”

But before the candidate could respond, we heard the sound of a metal-on-metal crunch, followed by a second crash. Across the street, a pickup truck had slammed into the cars on either side of it in an attempt to get out of a curb parking space. As I watched, the pickup hit the bumper of the car behind it again. The pickup was not parked in that tightly, so the driver must have been drunk. With one final sideswipe, the pickup cleared the cars and made its way into the street. I hadn’t noticed, but the candidate had run out in front of the pickup and now put up his hands. The driver honked, but the candidate stayed there, blocking him, with his hands raised. The driver leaned on the horn, and the candidate responded by slamming his fists down on the hood of the pickup. The driver jumped out of the pickup and ran right up to the candidate, screaming “Get out of my way!”

The candidate held his ground and screamed back. “You just hit two cars. You can’t drive.”

“Get you—you get out of my way!” The driver pushed the candidate, who held his ground. Then the driver wound up to take a punch. The candidate saw it coming. He stepped back so that the punch missed and then the candidate landed a huge uppercut to the driver’s jaw. The driver fell to the ground unconscious. The candidate picked the driver up like a baby and carried him back into the pickup. Then he took the keys out of the ignition, closed the door, and threw the keys high onto the roof of the adjacent building. It had all happened in seconds.

The candidate turned to me, cupped his hands and shouted across the street, “Some people just don’t know how to behave decent.”

Then he waved goodbye and walked toward the hotel. Snow continued falling, flake after flake on an altered landscape.

Twins

Jan LaPerle

At the McDonald's drive-thru my husband
told me about the Siamese twins, how one

twin woke one morning and his brother
in the night had died and he knew he was

soon to follow. I can't shake the feeling
of how I imagine that to feel and I was only

there getting an iced coffee. In these situations
I do not think of the Lord, though I know a lady

who does—she's on my mail route and some days
she talks so long I have to drive away smiling

as she's still talking and she talks of the Lord
like trust were as easy as the wind lifting

the flap of hair on her head that exposes
not the inch of gray hair pushing the red dye

north, but something I ought to look away from.
Wouldn't it be easier just to take her along

on my mail route, my arm on the sill browning
like a loaf and I wouldn't need the radio

just her monologues I'd interrupt only to ask
her to hand me a package, each marked with a number

like our days, and maybe she'd pee in the road with me;
maybe I'd teach her to build a quick stall with two

open doors and how to shove the used T.P. into an empty
Ziploc where my sandwiches used to live. It is her

with her hair, yes, lifting like a tent flap and her
dresses like tent flaps, too, who will walk with me

if we break down. Will she have an answer to why
the Lord didn't put his hand on the car there

now in the ditch, yes, so it'll be nice to walk with
her, it'll seem holy somehow the two of us

and with her I feel I could almost really believe
in more than just the beauty of the open road.

The calves frolicking in the far fields,
the wildflowers pushing up like crazy alongside

all these speeding cars swerving not to hit us
and the wildfires that burn the next town over,

we'll walk toward those, so full of the Lord,
together, they'll be sure to think we're twins.

Anesthesia

Jan LaPerle

Leaves and petals attend me. I am ready. —Sylvia Plath

For weeks it hasn't rained months
now all night I water the gardens
the fig tree the mosquitoes

holding hands laying me down
in the grasses not gently
quietly I cannot get up

I should have let the sun heal me
me with my tubes tied
around my neck and my daughter

watching horses watching clouds
only cartoon rain falling
asleep backwards into a hole

the nurse did nothing to keep me
here she seems not to like me
either I wake and I am nothing

look now how powerless I am
against drought against the bed
curtains and ceiling tiles

I feel their movement around me
but cannot see anyone
I do not want this to be

the nightmare I think it is
in the waiting room the ladies
file in each one as pregnant
as explosive everything pointed
toward me in the corner my ears
covered I hear them in there

screaming to get out they know
what I've done they are scared
there are no chairs left

no one calls for anyone
the only sound the secretaries
ringing telephones this room

their window they shut
behind curtains they've sewn
my lips closed because they know

the nurses who seemed at first
so friendly so quickly turned so
my friends and their effacement

look as clouds part as they pass
their hospital caps may never
rain they are tucking

me in tight and rolling me away
no one has told me where
my arms are strapped and my legs

we are rolling past windows now
each one a different day
different weather rain sun

burning so bright the grasses
browning now around the terrible
flowers stretching hard toward the sun

their petals all aflame.

Somewhere

Jan LaPerle

Early spring and only the crocuses,
morning and my work shirt, the one
with daisies, grasses so real when I stood
over my daughter to wake her, in her half-dream
I grew, a cloud of wildflowers she reached for.
She came away with nothing, and I've been away,
too many hotel breakfasts, too many people
waiting for their waffles—I can barely see them,
my Styrofoam plate too thin to hold what I need.
I am only one standing in line behind the others
looking down. I hold hands with my daughter
as we walk; I do not know if it is my sweat
or hers between us, a little pool, an ecosystem—
what is growing there? What am I letting
seep into her? In the shower she pulls
on her nipples, "when will I become a woman,"
she asks, the look on her face so far from me.
Today I met a soldier who once drove over
a little girl the size of his own—he had to,
to save himself, to save a hundred others.
My daughter today will stand on the edge
of the high-dive, even though I warned her,
and then she'll jump. The clouds reflected there
will pass beneath all those faces in the pool
like moons looking up through the branches
I stand beneath, where I holler, "I am no longer
afraid of you," and I believe because I have to.

Phyllis

Robert Rickelman

After the *desmadre* with Dad and Caryn, I once again had no place to live. My brother Kerry had a friend, Richard, who allowed me to sleep on his couch, provided I stayed sober.

I moved in on Thursday, November 20. Within two days, I'd finished all of Richard's alcohol, which consisted of a full fifth of vodka and an almost-full liter of what turned out to be some very expensive tequila.

On Saturday morning, I was confronted by a very angry Richard and told that I had one hour to pack my things and move out. I called my brother Kevin and asked him to help me out. Again.

Kevin picked me up at noon. He said he didn't have much money, and I didn't blame him for his reluctance to front me any cash. But he didn't know what else to do with me. Against his better judgment, he agreed to lend me three hundred dollars. I swore up and down that I would use the money only for food and rent, I would not buy any alcohol. Kevin wasn't an idiot, and I knew he didn't believe me, but he was giving me one last chance to do the right thing. He let me know that this would be the last money he would give me, and I knew I'd have to find a job quickly. Before the money ran out.

As far as my accommodations, Kevin suggested the seedy Gaslamp area, just south of downtown San Diego and within our budget. We drove downtown, and to the Gaslamp, where there was no shortage of seedy SRO's. I looked out my window, surveying the denizens of this bleak, decaying neighborhood. There were other drunks not unlike me, hookers, and a handful of disabled vets, flying their cardboard signs, asking for handouts, spare change, and such. These were my brethren. It was hard to imagine a drearier place to live.

The hotels, in their sorry condition, reminded me of my days at the Baywood, a similarly seamy hotel where I spent several alcohol-soaked months living in Chicago's rundown Ravenswood area. There was a time, after I'd moved out of the Baywood, that I landed a good job and put together a few months of sobriety. I missed those days.

Kevin found a parking space in front of a drab, gray, three-story building, the Prince Albert. It had probably once been a nice place, but that would have been many years ago.

While Kevin waited in the car, I got out and walked up the stairs of the hotel and through the main entrance. There were two steel doors on either side of the small foyer, one probably for the boiler room, and the other, perhaps a supply room. The front desk was one floor up. I opened a second door and walked quickly upstairs. I didn't want to keep Kevin waiting.

Once upstairs, I approached the front-desk clerk. He was a big, bald-headed guy in a dirty white T-shirt that highlighted not only his big round belly, but also some exceptionally large biceps. He was a very intimidating, no-nonsense guy. And he needed a shave.

I hadn't had a drink since the day before, and was feeling extremely anxious. I wished I could have had a few drinks to help me get through this. But Kevin had absolutely refused to stop and buy me some beer. I'd have to do this sober. Sober and shaky.

The clerk, whose name was Frank, told me that a week's rent was $60, and was expected on time, no exceptions, no excuses, no charity.

I told Frank that I'd be right back, and ran downstairs to get the money from Kevin. This would pay the rent for another week or two, and leave me some cash for liquor and food. I could not imagine life in this flophouse without a good, strong buzz.

I thanked Kevin, said my good-byes, grabbed my things, and rushed back upstairs to pay Frank my first week's rent. Frank gave me my key and pointed out my room. Shit, I thought, I'm only a few doors from the desk. Well, I reasoned, maybe being near the front desk would mean less noise at night.

After I checked in, I went to my room. It was more dismal than the Baywood. Everything was dingy and smoke-covered, and the bed was a twin-size with a rusty metal frame and a thin, worn mattress.

Against the wall was an old wooden desk and a rickety chair with dirty, orange, threadbare upholstery. Just like the Baywood's, the sink had a hot faucet and a cold one. And like the Baywood's, the sink would also double as my urinal.

I walked down the hall to check the bathroom; it was moldy, smelly, and generally disgusting. I imagined that somebody had taken a nasty shit just before I walked in.

But I had to stay positive. I would get a job and move out of this dump as soon as I could. For now, though, with Kevin gone, it was time to get some alcohol. So I left my second-floor hovel in search of a cheap liquor store.

I found a place that catered to winos. That meant they sold fortified, or screw-cap, wine, better known as bum wine, with catchy names like Mad Dog, Thunderbird, and Night Train. They also carried a selection of 40-ounce bottles of malt liquor, which contained more alcohol than regular beer. I bought a 40-ouncer, an eighteen-pack of cheap beer, and two fifths of low-end vodka, which was probably one rung above rubbing alcohol.

The liquor store also sold ramen noodles for 50¢ a package, which was a rip-off. I had no stove, so I would sprinkle the seasoning on the noodles and eat them dry. They actually tasted pretty good that way. I bought four packs of ramen and headed back to the hotel.

As I passed the front desk I wondered if Frank noticed, or even cared, about the eighteen-pack and the heavy brown grocery bag I was carrying.

I estimated that the alcohol I'd bought would be enough to last me two or three days as long as I didn't get crazy and drink it all up. I would have to conserve it, drinking just enough to keep my head straight and my courage high. Monday I would start my job search.

I didn't want to waste my money on the price of a Sunday paper, so I'd have to find a copy or read one at the library. I would worry about that tomorrow. For now, it was time to calm my nerves with some drinks.

I quickly opened and drank two cans of beer to steady my nerves, then poured a few ounces of warm vodka into a glass. The vodka burned as it passed down my throat. I needed the buzz and savored the burn.

I lay down on the bed and looked at my watch. It was 3:00 p.m., November 22, 1986, the start of my exciting new life in downtown San Diego. I thought to myself how Thanksgiving was just days away. But this year it would simply be another date on the calendar. I opened the 40-ouncer and emptied it within twenty minutes. I drifted slowly to sleep.

When I awoke, the room was dark. There was some faint light filtering in from the parking lot next door. It was just after midnight. I drank a beer, then poured myself a bit of vodka and fell back to sleep.

I awoke Sunday morning at 6:15. The sun hadn't fully risen, and the room was still dark. It was time for a beer. I popped one open and drank it quickly. I was surprised to have acquired a craving for an orange soda. There was a vending machine on the street corner, but I'd need a few ounces of vodka before I could leave my room. I poured myself half a glass and drained it.

The vodka burned harsher than I'd expected, so I cupped my hand and drank some tepid water from the cold-water faucet. I sat on the bed, relishing the early morning buzz that warmed my gut and soothed my soul.

Feeling sufficiently composed, I opened my door and was surprised to see a young woman, petite, probably Hispanic and very pretty. She had coal-black eyes that matched her raven-dark, shoulder-length hair. Her bangs were short, as if she'd cut them herself. But oddly, the short bangs accentuated her lovely olive skin.

She wore a pink cotton halter, white shorts that showed a lot of leg, and a pair of yellow rubber thong sandals. Although her features were exquisite, she looked exhausted. Not so much lack-of-sleep tired, more world-weary and languid.

And then there were the bruises. Her arms and legs bore several painful-looking red and purple blotches. She even had one on her face, high on her forehead, partially hidden by her bangs. I didn't know much about HIV or AIDS, but that's what I figured was the reason for so many patches of discolored skin.

She met my gaze and smiled. "Good morning, you must be new here."

She had probably just finished working the street.

I smiled. "Good morning. Yeah, you're right, I just moved in yesterday." I tried to act as sober as possible, and, actually, by my standards, I wasn't all that drunk.

"Well, hi, I'm Phyllis. I've been here since June."

I did some quick math and reckoned that she had been living there for six months. A half a year in this fucking dump.

"Hi, Phyllis. I'm Rob. Pleased to meet you."

Phyllis had a sweet disposition that made me instantly fond of her. "So, Rob, what brings you to the luxurious Prince Albert Hotel?"

"I'm here for the ambiance." I grinned nervously. Boy, that was lame. "Umm… actually, I'm a little tight on funds," I said.

"Don't I know it. Well this place isn't really as bad as it looks. There are three desk clerks, Dora and Alfredo are real nice. I guess you met Frank yesterday. He's a big asshole. And he doesn't take any shit, especially when the rent's due. He doesn't cut anyone any slack. Just a warning, ya know?"

"Frank. Yeah, thanks. You're right. He wasn't all that charming when I checked in."

Phyllis laughed. "Charming? Nope, charming is definitely not a word I would use to describe Frank."

"Well, I'm heading downstairs to get a can of pop," I said.

"Pop, huh? Chicago?"

"Yeah, I guess I mean soda."

"No I like the way you Chicago people say pop."

"Where are you from?" I asked.

"San Diego, born and raised. Local kid makes good." She smiled wanly. It was a joke, but it wasn't funny. She knew it wasn't funny.

"Well ... um ... can I get you anything? A soda?"

"Yeah, ya know, a Dr Pepper would really hit the spot. Here's a buck. The machine is 50¢, use the change to get yourself one."

"Thanks, but you don't have to do that."

"Hey, you're doing me a favor. I want to do a favor for you."

"Thanks, I'll be right back."

As I headed down the stairs, I couldn't take my mind off the lesions. I wondered if she was dying. AIDS was still a formidable disease back in the '80s, and to my untrained eye, her case looked fairly well advanced. I wondered how her customers, her Johns, could overlook her very obvious bruising. Were they that desperate to get laid?

I walked to the corner and stopped at the soda machine. I put in a dollar bill and pressed Dr Pepper. A can dropped down the chute, and two quarters fell into the change holder. I put them into the coin slot, pressed Orange Crush, and my can dropped down with a thud.

I walked back to the hotel and up the stairs. Phyllis was still there, smoking a cigarette. A Marlboro. She offered me one.

"No, thanks. Smoking's probably the only bad habit I don't have." I handed her the Dr Pepper.

"Bad habit? Gee, thanks."

I blushed. I appreciated her sense of humor. She was sweet, but I'm sure she had to be pretty fucking tough to be a hooker in this rundown area, or anywhere for that matter.

"Yeah, I can thank my dad for that. When I was twelve, my nine-year-old brother and I asked my dad if we could smoke a cigar. He said sure, under one condition: Once Keith, my brother, and I lit our cigar, we had to smoke the whole thing.

"We couldn't believe that our dad had actually said yes. So we rushed to the corner store and bought two Parodi cigars, I think we paid a buck for the two of them. They looked like stubby little Slim Jims.

"We were back home in no time. Our dad told us to smoke them in the back yard. He didn't want us smelling up the house with cigar smoke. He lit the cigars for us, and we started puffing away. We actually inhaled them like we'd seen our mom do when she smoked her cigarettes. We didn't know you weren't supposed to inhale cigars.

"Our dad chuckled, 'Enjoy your cigars. Let me know when you're finished.'

"We didn't even get halfway through and we were both puking our guts out. Our dad heard the noise and came outside.

'You haven't finished your cigars, guys. Is there a problem?'

'Please, Dad. We're so sick. Can't we stop?'

'Okay, here's the deal. You can stop smoking, but I don't ever want you to see you smoking anything again. Cigars, pipes, cigarettes. Nothing.'

'Okay, Dad,' we promised amidst our heaving.

'Stay out here until you feel better. Do your puking outside.'

"Then he walked into the house laughing. But you know what? That killed the smoking bug for me… well… until pot."

"And your brother?"

I laughed, "You know what? He smokes cigars and a pipe. He's a better man than I am."

She laughed. I hoped I'd cheered her up. "Well, Mr. Parodi, that was quite a tale. Now I've got to get some sleep. Thanks for the pop."

"Soda," I corrected her.

Phyllis laughed. "Soda."

I hoped she wasn't dying.

ABDUCTED
Ian Andrew Young
acrylic on canvas
36x36

DR. MARIO
Ian Andrew Young
acrylic on canvas
24x30

Guess Whos
Ian Andrew Young
acrylic on canvas
48x48

Raising Antiope

Clemonce Heard

& when my princess grew too spacious
to fit the Goodwill gown I purchased,

we turned it into a sun dress. Once the
straps began to strangle my sweet-pea

we made it a sweetheart, hit puberty
a halter top, hit her head on the ceiling

a cropped top. Whenever she outgrew
the house she stopped sporting her

charmeuse as a scarf & wore it instead
as a hijab, which are both fine by me

since neither is a bikini. When her veil
began to choke her face we made it

into a headband, & when that failed a
scrunchie, to keep her ponytail in place.

Sinkhole

Cara Rodriguez

Once there was a corner house with shingles that were coming up, but that didn't seem to matter. In the evening people came and brought menudo and posole, mole and tamales, and the house was warm and yellow and the couches were torn and both mariachi radio and chicken bones sat on the counter. When thick smog-like jowls came early in the morning, a bucket of water would be dumped out on the front cement and the trash from the day before swept into the street with a straw broom.

Once there was an intersection outside the corner house where cars slowed and drivers waved to one another. Sometimes two cars would stop there, right in the middle of the road, and the drivers would talk to one another through rolled down windows, elbows and shoulders leaning out. Mufflers, heavy with engine rumble, a cigar in one hand, laughter under moustache—these mingled with the scent of old mango peels dotted with chili powder tossed on the ground the night before.

And then a hole opened.

The surface gave way under the weight of an unexpected breeze. The walkway to the house now under the ground, crumbled among dark tunnels. People gathered and stared. "How do we get to the house?" they asked. "What can be done?" There began a slow trembling in the leaves of limon trees in the yards. Wooden planks were brought out and arranged but the boards were too shaky. No one wanted to fall in. No matter the rain, the hole never became a milky-eyed pool they could swim across. Children with ratted hair drew pictures of what the street used to look like and dropped them into the hole and sat and waited for the street to remember.

One by one, heads turned from the house and began to stare, instead, at the volcanoes edging the city. "Less dangerous," women whispered. Men drank coffee and tequila at tables in silence. They all found reasons to walk other streets: The best oranges were on another block. "There is still bus exhaust," they would say, "and there is always the smell of bread from the four corner bakeries."

Pigeons still fly overhead and land in the plazas and do not say a word, and the garbage man comes each day, ringing his heavy bell.

Rockhound

Cara Rodriguez

I huddled next to the glowing coils
of the space heater
in my father's workshop.
He taught me about rocks and minerals,
        the translucent rust blocks of rutile,
        green tourmaline,
        jade and granite and garnet,
        the deceit of pyrite.
He taught me how to gather them,
label them,
showed me what part of the mineral I could touch
and where my small fingers
would break the crystals.

On weekends I hunted
the hills and cliffs on the edge
of town. At recess I devoured
the school yard, searching,
digging. Dusting off agate
and petrified wood,
I pressed my thumb against
their cool round edges,
until I felt their secret pulse.
I cupped calcite in my hand
        and heard its whisper
                be sensitive,
held quartz up to the sun
crying, *Variety! Variety!*

squinting as the light came through.

I filled my pockets,
held the small teachers tight
in my palms,
and when there was no more space,
they were shoved into my backpack,
next to a peanut butter and honey sandwich.

As I grow older
rock, stone
and mineral appear in
odd places—in my bed, my shoes,
they are brushed from my hair.
They glint in
words spoken around me,
(galena's warning
                    experience will taint you).
Dense, crystal boxes of light and lie,
and thick, jagged angles
of hard argument
fall from my fingers and
scatter along the ground where I walk.

I hold a piece of schist,
pick at the tight layers,
and think, "This is my brother,"
or myself.

The earth's crust is
12% quartz.
When I move I am aware of what is
beneath my feet,
those clear and foggy points
of what I thought were diamonds.

Mimeo Paternity

Roberta P. Feins

Machine in the back office, where
someone strong and manly cranked the handle.
Paper thrust out each cycle,
shiny wet with purple ink, smelling
like seaweed and cotton candy.

A stencil, shackled to the drum, birthed copies
without a moan. No woman, easily bruised,
bleeding bright red ink. Pallid letters.

Thirty copies, multiple choice, studded
with question marks. I was the last copy,
spat out before he crumpled the battered stencil.

Ink gleaming on his hands, my father
held me up to dry. He knew what the copies
should say. No time to re-cut the stencil,
hope for a boy.

Downtown Kansas Ave.
Harvey Flowers
photography
10x10

TOPEKA SANTA FE AMTRAK STATION
Harvey Flowers
photography
10x10

Fear of Heights

Ellen Birkett Morris

When she heard Tony died, Allison thought of his hands, the way they had danced palm to palm when they were dating. She remembered the night he put his fingers through hers. It made her think of the children's game where you formed the church and steeple with your hands.

"Marry me," he'd whispered.

To her surprise, she said yes.

That was years ago. She had since come to believe that love was a beautiful and spiky thing.

Allison went into the backyard where Lydia was bent over a patch of poppies, pulling up weeds.

"We're going to Slocum."

Lydia sat up on her heels and raised her eyebrows.

"Tony died."

Lydia got to her feet and went over to put her arms around Allison. They stood in the garden together, the oversweet smell of hyacinth in the air.

Lydia and Allison lived just outside of Cincinnati, which seemed like New York City after Slocum. There were German delicatessens, Unitarian churches, and art house cinemas that showed foreign movies.

The drive to Slocum was just over two hours. The highway between Cincinnati and Slocum was all fields and horse farms, except Florence with its brightly colored tower with *Florence Y'all* painted on the side. Lydia drove while Allison looked out the window.

Lydia relished the time away from the endless parade of students with their issues and questions. She was nearing her retirement and would be relieved not to have to break up arguments between kids anymore or hear their cruel taunts. She worried that the next school counselor might not know how to handle the girls whose mothers didn't prepare them for their menses. She had a cabinet stocked with pamphlets, pads, and tampons and a chart she showed the girls to explain their cycle. She was sure to tell them that there could be headaches or bloating and that they were liable to feel sad or irritable. She never called it a blessing or a curse. It was what it was.

Allison let her mind wander from her eighth grade class at Walnut Hills High School to Tony. She rarely thought of Slocum. But sometimes in her classroom after school, when the sunlight hit the cabinets just right, she recalled Tony's hand on the small of her back and remembered how safe he had made her feel. With Lydia everything was mirrored, the pitch of their voices, the curve of their bodies, the softness of their skin.

Her betrayal of Tony years ago was like a cold front that came up unexpectedly, chilling the air between her and Lydia, and leaving Allison numb. She hated distance between them. When they reached the outskirts of Slocum, Allison reached over to hold Lydia's free hand. Lydia ran her thumb slowly across Allison's palm.

*

The first time Lydia saw Allison, she was wheeling a film projector crookedly through the hallway.

"The wheel is turned around," Lydia said. "I can fix it." She knelt and turned the wheel so that it faced forward. She saw Allison's delicate ankles above her red pumps, the bone a tender pyramid that made her think of places far more exotic than Slocum Junior High.

She took a moment to compose herself and returned to her feet.

"I'm Allison Conti. I don't think we've met." Allison extended her hand.

Lydia noticed that Allison had small fine wrists to match her ankles and a shiny gold wedding band. Her husband was Tony Conti, a carpenter.

Lydia imagined her hands encircling Allison's wrists. As they stood in the hallway talking about the upcoming break, Allison ran her hand slowly through her hair.

Allison had wanted a best girlfriend, someone to talk to, cook with and share secrets with. Most of her old high school friends were immersed in having children. Their conversational repertoire ranged from infant sleep habits to the merits of breast feeding. Babies didn't interest her. She liked kids around the age of ten, when they started having opinions about things. She liked how earnest and hopeful they were, how unafraid to share their thoughts.

Allison couldn't imagine being a mother. She still felt like a kid herself, newly married, first real job. She loved substitute teaching—geometry problems one day, the life cycle of a frog the next. The kids were funny. School was where she felt fully adult, fully in charge, until she met Lydia.

Lydia was the counselor. She had a private office and kept a journal with her wherever she went. She had blond hair, a strong chin, and the most melancholy eyes Allison had ever seen.

As their friendship grew, Lydia knew she would have to move slowly. She was sure Allison felt the electricity between them and that it confused her. She didn't want to scare Allison away. Still, she took every opportunity to touch Allison when they spent time together after school. She'd grab Allison's arm when a scene got tense at the movies.

Once, after school on the way to her car, Allison dropped a pile of homework papers and they blew in all directions. She and Lydia chased the papers across the parking lot laughing and screaming until they got every last one. Then Lydia threw her arms around Allison and their laughter stopped. Allison's face got serious and Lydia tugged playfully on Allison's collar.

"You have to be more careful, clumsy girl," said Lydia.

Allison felt a flutter in her stomach.

*

It was their ritual. Every Sunday evening, Tony and Allison walked hand in hand through the graveyard, which was enclosed by a brick wall. Allison's mother was buried there and each week they brought a fresh bouquet to lay at the grave site. They walked the gravel paths, rested on the stone benches and admired the towering oak trees. In the middle of the yard, there was a gazebo with a swing. It was ringed by tea roses. They sat down.

"How are the cabinets for Goodies coming?"

"They're coming along. Solid oak with turned corners and long plates of glass for the kids to press their noses against."

"So Abby is happy with them?"

"Sure, why wouldn't she be?"

"She's picky, Tony." She found Tony's friend to be cold and critical.

"She's discerning," he said. "How are things at school?"

"I'm going to fill in for Sue Johansson when she goes on maternity leave."

"Her room is close to Lydia's office. You won't have to go so far to visit."

"We don't visit during school."

"I drove by just last week and saw you all eating lunch under the big oak."

"It was Lydia's birthday. I just brought a few sandwiches and cupcakes."

"I love that you have a best friend. I know you still miss your mom. It's good to have someone besides me to share things with."

"I don't need anyone else to share things with," said Allison.

"What has you so grumpy tonight?" asked Tony, pulling Allison close. For the first time ever, Allison felt like pushing him away.

*

Lydia lived in a small frame house on the edge of town. It was close enough to the railroad tracks that she could hear the train's low lonely whistle as it went through town each night at 11:30. She told Allison that she loved the quiet after a noisy day at school.

Allison was surprised by how spare the place was. A couch, low wooden coffee table and lawyer bookshelf occupied the living room. A small glass globe with ribbons of purple inside sat on the windowsill.

A single bed with a white iron frame, a wooden dresser, and an old-fashioned rocker were the only furniture in the bedroom. "My nun's chamber," joked Lydia. A picture on the wall showed a tired looking woman in a backyard holding a baby. The yard was overgrown with weeds and in the corner you could see the edge of an old settee.

"We lived outside of Pikeville," said Lydia. "Three rooms, five kids, no running water. I never would have escaped if it wasn't for the Berea College student work program."

"Were you the oldest?"

"The oldest girl, which made me chief bottle washer and babysitter. I applied for school in secret. The librarian let me use her address. I snuck out in the middle of the night and she drove me to Berea. It was the only way I was getting out."

"Did your family come looking for you?"

"No."

“Did you ever go back?”

“No.”

The teakettle whistled.

“Sit down,” said Allison. Lydia watched her drop in the tea bags into the cup and pour the water on top. She wanted this moment to last forever.

*

When she felt bad for Tony, Lydia reminded herself that Allison kissed her first. They were hiking in Blenheim Forest down a trail that led to a fire tower overlooking the woods. The sun shone through the canopy making pools of light on the forest floor. Lydia stopped Allison to show her an iridescent bug on the side of a tree. A small green snake slithered across the path. When Allison stumbled on a rock, Lydia steadied her.

At the tower, stairs zigzagged up the interior of the steel tower to a room above. They made their way slowly up the stairs. When they reached the top, they stood in a small room with views of the forest below, Lake Devon and the mountains in the distance.

“Breathtaking, isn’t it?” said Lydia.

“Yeah,” said Allison, gasping for air.

“Are you OK?”

“Fear of heights,” said Allison.

“You should have told me.”

“I didn’t want to spoil the fun,” Allison said with a laugh.

Lydia took her hand and pulled Allison to the center of the room.

"From right here you can't even tell we're up high," said Lydia, putting her arms around Allison as they faced each other. "Everything is good right here, right?"

"Yeah," said Allison.

Lydia felt Allison's heart beat fast against her own.

"Let's go a bit closer," said Lydia.

They moved in a slow dance until they reached the rail.

Lydia turned Allison toward the rail, keeping her hands around Allison's waist.

"I've got you," said Lydia. "I won't let anything happen."

While Allison looked out over the forest, Lydia buried her nose in Allison's hair.

They stood in silence; the only sound was the wind blowing through the trees below.

Allison turned around and looked up at Lydia, her eyes soft.

"How am I ever going to get down off of here?"

"One step at a time," said Lydia.

Allison leaned close and kissed her lightly on the lips.

When Lydia pulled her close, Allison willed her to move her hands up onto her breasts, but Lydia held her gently around the waist. Finally, they heard footfalls on the steps and parted.

That night in bed Allison imagined herself and Lydia intertwined, pressed hard against the rail, while in the forest below tiny fires burned away, leaving bare, dark ground.

*

Allison watched Tony sand the kitchen cabinets, his hand moving back and forth in perfect rhythm. She was sick over her betrayal. She couldn't stop replaying the moment when her lips met Lydia's, her surprise at how right it all felt. Allison had wanted that kiss and more. It reminded her of the time she pulled out into traffic at the last minute and a truck narrowly missed hitting her car. The sound of the horn made her heart beat faster and for a moment she felt more alive, more awake than she had ever been.

She turned to the window. Outside the buds were coming out on the dogwood tree. Bits of green grass were sprouting on the lawn. She felt a lump rise in her throat.

She turned to Tony. He looked up at her.

"Are you all right?"

"I wouldn't hurt you for the world."

Tony looked startled.

"What is it? What happened?"

"A kiss," she said, choking back sobs.

"Who is he? I'll make sure he never comes near you."

"It was Lydia. I think I love her."

Tony looked at her in disbelief. Allison reached out to touch Tony and he stepped back, out of range.

Allison left the kitchen and went into the backyard. The yard was edged with flowerbeds, freshly tilled dirt that had been sprinkled with seeds the week before. She wouldn't be around to see them bloom.

She went back into the kitchen at dusk. Tony looked up and offered a conciliatory smile.

"You'll be back," he said with certainty. He had done this before, acted as if she didn't know her own mind and she had surrendered to it, but not now. It would be easy to stay and succumb to the warmth and security he offered, to his goodness. She wanted more.

She packed a small bag. When she returned to the kitchen, Tony was where she had left him. She walked over and kissed him on the cheek.

Tony didn't move. He stayed there, sandpaper in hand, as he heard the front door close.

He saw her small footprint in the dust; a draft could blow it away. All it would take was one gust of the spring breeze.

*

Lydia went to see Tony at his jobsite at the Hansen place. Seth Hansen had died of old age and his niece Adrienne was redoing the house. She hadn't told Allison she was going, knowing that it would upset her. It would be the only time she had ever been alone in a room with Tony.

Lydia knocked on the half-open front door and walked into the foyer.

"Tony?"

"In here."

He knelt in front of the fireplace, a stack of bricks at his side as he laid a new hearth.

"Lydia, what could you possibly have to say to me?"

Lydia walked across the room and sat on the edge of the couch.

"We didn't mean for it to happen. It was just one kiss, but it meant something to us both."

"You seduced her. Did you know that she'd never been kissed when I met her? She was so shy. She lost her mom when she was ten. She's confusing love with something else."

"It's not like that. Some people are just wired differently. They need something else," Lydia said gently.

"It's something else all right," said Tony.

He bent his head and continued laying the bricks and filling in the space between them with cement. Each one was perfectly placed. It was so quiet that after a while Lydia noticed the branch of a holly tree scratching at the window. She took one last look at Tony on his knees and left.

*

Allison returned to Tony's house one afternoon to get her things. She was surprised to see his truck in the driveway. Inside she saw that he had painted all the walls taupe, the coral living room, the yellow kitchen, and the forest-green sunroom.

Through the kitchen window, she saw Tony in the backyard digging a small square patch of land. They had talked about planting a garden this year. Now it would grow without her charting its progress. She imagined plants bending over with the weight of lush tomatoes, mounds of spinach low to the ground, and flowering sage along the edges.

She climbed the stairs and found her suitcase packed and three cardboard boxes marked *Allison*. There was no trace of her anywhere in the room; the vanity was bare and the closet held only Tony's clothes.

She heard his footsteps on the stairs. She walked further into the room and held onto the bedpost. The bed, its headboard carved with vines and roses, was his present to her when they married.

"You found your things?"

"Yes. Thank you for packing them."

"Now you can take them and go."

"I won't even have to unpack. We're moving to Cincinnati."

"In a big city like that nobody will think twice about two bachelor girls living together."

"Sarcasm doesn't become you, Tony. You're one of the sweetest people I know."

"I'm not that man anymore. Not after this."

"I know you're hurting."

"You don't know a thing about me," he said. He picked up two of the boxes and headed down the stairs. Allison took the other box and the suitcase.

He placed the boxes carefully in the trunk of her car. She stood with her back against the car. He came to her and placed his palms against hers, his fingers through her own.

"Allison," he said, his chin resting on her head.

"Tony," she replied. His tears landed on the top of her head like an unexpected rain.

*

Tony had a plain wooden coffin, nothing polished or carved. Allison stood by Lydia's side, holding her upper arm tightly. She wouldn't hold Lydia's hand here, everyone would talk.

"By the end, he had forgotten everything," said Abby Linder. "He was like a baby."

Allison remembered the sweet man she had loved, his kindness, the beautiful things he had created. Lydia passed her a linen handkerchief. Years as a counselor had taught Lydia when to keep her mouth shut.

After the funeral they went to the diner and ordered pieces of banana cream pie with towering meringue. There is nothing a little sugar can't fix, Lydia's mother used to say. Lydia knew it wasn't true, then or now. She remembered the blueberry cobbler her mother would make each time she learned she was pregnant again with another child for Lydia to help raise. Lydia and her mother would sit at the kitchen table with two spoons and eat the entire pan.

*

As they rode down the highway past the white wooden fences and horse barns, Allison placed her hand in her pocket and ran her finger across the figure of a small long stemmed rose with one tiny thorn carved out of its side. Abby had given it to her. Tony had carved it. When Abby had come to visit Tony months before he died he had presented it to her and said, "I made this for you, Allison."

Abby said she had taken Tony's hands in hers and said, "Thank you. It's lovely."

Allison put her hand in her pocket and felt the thorn sharp against her finger. She drew her hand away and placed it on her lap. She was staring out the window when she felt Lydia's hand find her own.

THE KITCHEN CAT (FOR STUART DAVIS)
David Lee Quick
acrylic on canvas
48x36

"The painting is a meditation on the birth, life, death, and afterlife of carrots."

Wig
David Lee Quick
acrylic/collage/assemblage on paper board
12x16

"The work is an homage to the all-encompassing multimedia stylizations of John Cage."

He Blew It All to Hell
David Lee Quick
acrylic on chalk board
16x20

"The painting is an elegy regarding the death of Jean-Michel Basquiat."

Russula Crenulata

Dawn Hogue

Nearly a week of rain
has given life to spores
settled in the spring soil,
and this morning's early light
reveals a mushroom, bright white
against the lawn's green edge.
Genus Russula is most common,
though I would not tell her that,
the little slight-stemmed lady
in her Elizabethan collar
cupping the morning dew
in her upturned cap.
Her visit will be
brief enough.

Irrelevant Thoughts Going Through My Head During an Intimate Moment

Matthue Roth

1. Hamtramck: A city (pronounced "Ham-trannick") that's actually located inside, and surrounded by, the city of Detroit, Michigan. In the glory days of car manufacturing, it was a place for working-class people to commute from their jobs and exist with their families in a little bubble. I met a photographer a few years ago who lived there. These days it's become a hub for artists with ties to the automotive industry. He was an art photographer who paid his rent by taking pictures of new cars.

2. My agent, and how he just called, and how late I am with my book, and how lucky I am that he's asking about my book at all instead of just writing me off.

3. My grandmother. She had a scab on her toe that she ignored because she thought it was, you know, a scab. She went to see a doctor and they told her they had to amputate. That should have happened today. I called her before the procedure, but not since, and I'm wondering how many toes she has at this moment.

4. The lyrics to the poem "Do not go gentle into that good night." It was the first, and so far the only, poem to ever stick in my head, except "in the room the women come and go / Talking of Michelangelo," which I hate admitting, partly because T.S. Eliot was such an anti-Semite, and partly that it's so close to *Cats,* the musical, which isn't fair to him, no matter what his occasionally racist philosophy, because he didn't ask for his poems to be twisted and excised and Broadway'd like that, and I'd just be doing the same thing all over again—although, to be fair to me, it *is* a chorus.

5. I want this to be the only thing I'm thinking about. When I have an experience, I want to experience it fully, to believe in you and not question a thing, nor be deterred by the other things in life, the more minor and insignificant things, like what I do all day and if it makes enough money and how to make that money pay for school and the house and any other things we might need in our life. Like, for example, the boxes of shoes that show up from the internet, more shoes than any of us could ever wear. I don't want to think about shoes. I want to think about nothing, not at all.

6. Your boobs.

7. How the rabbis tell us this is a holy experience, and I should have more faith, but the more I commit myself to the experience and go beyond the physical, the less I am moored in the experience itself. The more other thoughts begin creeping in, worries and concerns and, just, life.

The Things that Go Through My Head While I Pray

Matthue Roth

1. I bet the baby has a cucky in her diaper. I should not be holding her right now.

2. But no one else is awake, and raising kids is G-d's work, and making babies—*pru u'revu,* in the Torah—is a mitzvah, we're required to do it. We are required to have sex.

3. But the years that come after it, it is so hard.

4. The hidden Riddler trophies I still have yet to find in *Batman: Arkham Asylum*. There are 240 of them, and I've found, I think, 137? And I shouldn't care about finding them, but I do, and there's one I needed to rappel across the Batcave to get, and I didn't, but I could go back tonight. If I remember. If I remember.

5. Will the last chapter of my book ever end, or will I keep thinking of new things to add to it forever? The book is about a woman who turns her living room into the Holy Temple. It's impossible to pray and not think about writing it. It's impossible to write it and not think about praying.

6. I don't want to understand these words. I understand 25% of them, maybe 35% on a good day. I want to feel them, and believe them, and be them. I want to become nullified to the process. I want to be nothing.

7. But I can't clear my head of any of it. My doubt, my uncertainty, and my anxiety are parts of me, the parts of the prayer, and they're what make it different from any other person's prayer. Ani Difranco says, "My body is borrowed/I got it on loan/between my mother and a pile of maggots," and so are these words—there's no copyright; they don't belong to anyone but the universe. So here I am, wrestling with my body, wrestling with my space in the universe. Mounting that space. Filling it.

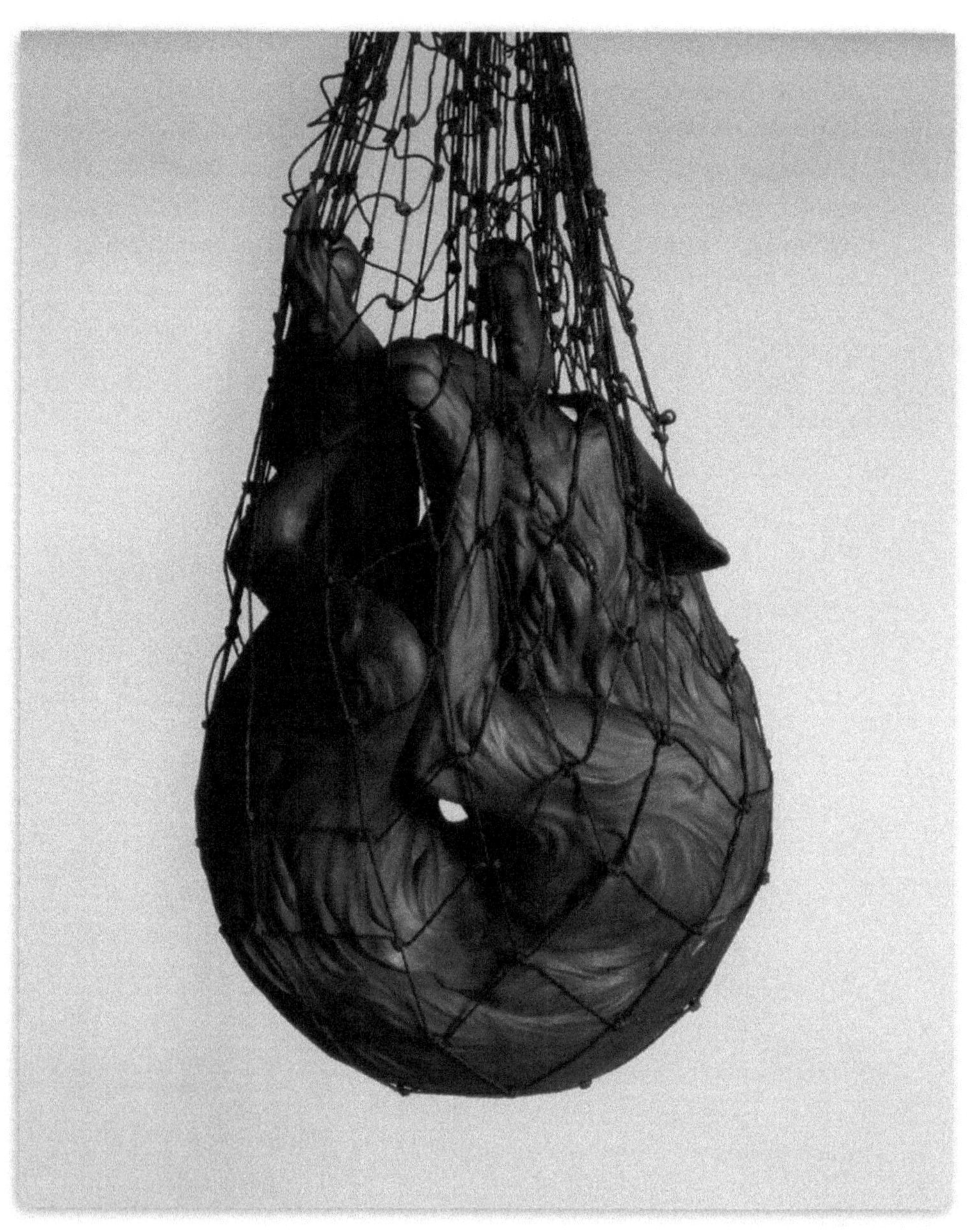

THE OPTIMIST
Tyler Quintin
ceramic, acrylic, hand-tied net
18x30x12

Cosmic Questions

Dianne Silvestri

I read of a man in Bosnia
who, rather than rant and curse,

purchased steel plates for his roof
after scientists verified

the sixth meteor strike in three years.
Experts cannot explain

this homing of galactic trash
to a tiny terrestrial target,

nor do they understand
why one of my cells turned killer.

Martian

James Cagney

After terraforming your night skin into a constellation of succulents
—what else is worth exploring? Tongue hostage / to new geophysic

language / magnetic fingers / in orbit spinning /sleep fidgeting
sticky dream nipples / hammocked in a star cluster across your lap

your black gibbous moons indecisive waxing, waning to & fro
chanting canticles of milk behind a firewall of jean fabric.

Their nutmeg fusion. Their viscous humidity, simmering
heady brine of skin. I encourage your body's ecstatic gasp

your emotive solo emptying bags of munitions across
radiant fields of sweet hair & bedspreads like any man at war.

Your fountains' loud spewing to the applause of rising pigeons—
every haunted chamber in your throat squeaking open—

my heart thumps to standstill, how a saluting soldier defers
to her superior. I am touch illiterate. I search for words

in my own mouth, my sweet & sour lunar crater. Despite
its post-apocalyptic emptiness. What word best describes an

appetite for the unknown? Don't say desire. Longing is
a pornographic surname in certain tribes. So, ... how to

translate a sonnet of moans? Guess the temperature of your
nearest stranger? What are you okay with just giving away?

You got me bout to come is how I begin all my prayers. You got me
curious about what arrives & what flavor it assumes. I could fast

on your stardust alone for 8 days, naming each molecule uniquely,
after jazz singers, animals, galaxy clusters. Your mouth could

revive me / tonguing my keyboard of nerves. Your soft valley of
new hairs string my upright spinal bass. Psychedelic flowers to

cultivate, weeping yeast for bread to bake. Your eyelashes &
lips bruise me from inside out. I am sticky & fibrous.

A moldy peach shattered by the kitchen floor. I am stone,
I am mop, I am swarm of sugared water / a bee shopping

the spires of the giant blue hyssop, lactating sugar.
            Do you know the origin for the word testimony?

Back then, words were valued that much. What makes
it really strange is how easy its legend is to believe. A row of

soldiers willing to exchange their balls if their word falls impotent.
Please note, history's second choice in oathing after *balls* is *bible*.

Perhaps Adam's balls were filled with the Word of God, or honey,
or sea water. Truth! Cross my heart, pumping like a dorm mattress.

He named each animal, but there's never been a proper name for
free range loneliness migrating head to toe. & what did Adam

eat? After naming each animal did he lick it, check its seasoning?
Who will feed us if we can't name what we want on a plate?

Fuck You, a waitress once yelled. *I'll need tabs of Viagra*
& an extension cord, I shouted back. I, a quasar light years from rapture,

sat in a spaceship alone as if waiting to be seen by an alien official.
I had no oath to swear, declare or sign. Not this pubic canopy, this

rainforest or its fresh & fruity antibiotics. Use me to keep warm
like how you once used a campfire. You'll need dry, fine tinder

& friction spinning & grinding to work the flame up the ladder;
Until embers awaken their bright red eyes & begin to weep smoke.

No one has touched me & triggered fire. No one has touched
me except to shove my shoulder as they rush past, blind.

If I remain in people's way, I shall be touched again. Even if
touch rhymes with choke, or burn or shove, it's still touch.

I see sex as a kind of conversation with various sticking points.
Yet my past lovers have been mutes with mouths full of mirrors

or judges who gavel on over guilt & sentences. How might you describe
your first love? Clumsy or clever? Stupid or selfish? Or sad, sad, sad?

The sun was first described as an erupting volcano falling from the sky.
Magmatic, hot to see, enflamed, brilliant, cast gold luminous &

swelling upon its approach, darkness parting in star-crested waves.
The sun itself described the flavor of darkness how one might explain

skin first tasted / skin not your own / foreign & savory its seasoned
cells sweating oyster water. Swallowed flames reheat the body's

forgotten science of wasted fertility. Then we whisper ourselves
clean, scrub our thighs with smoke /we shake, we hold, till its

time to let go. We emerge from shadows somehow more dumb
but at least relieved. The world remained the same, it was me

made glossy with newness & unanswerable questions. My life:
Unrested. Unloved. Undercover? No—alive & throbbing & alone

Untitled image from the project *Becoming a Specter*
Daniel W. Coburn
photograph/archival inkjet print
30x24

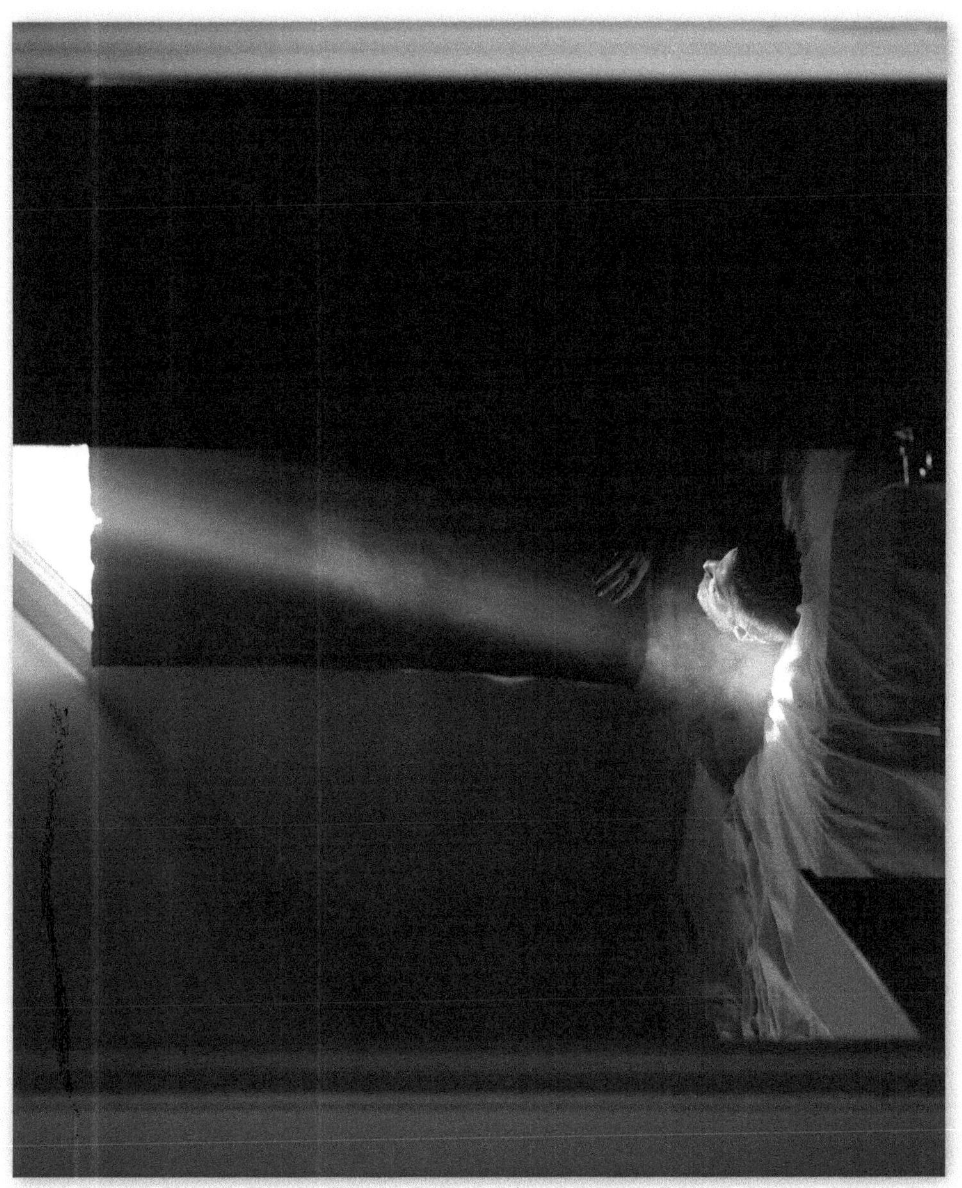

Untitled image from the project *Becoming a Specter*
Daniel W. Coburn
photograph/archival inkjet print
30x24

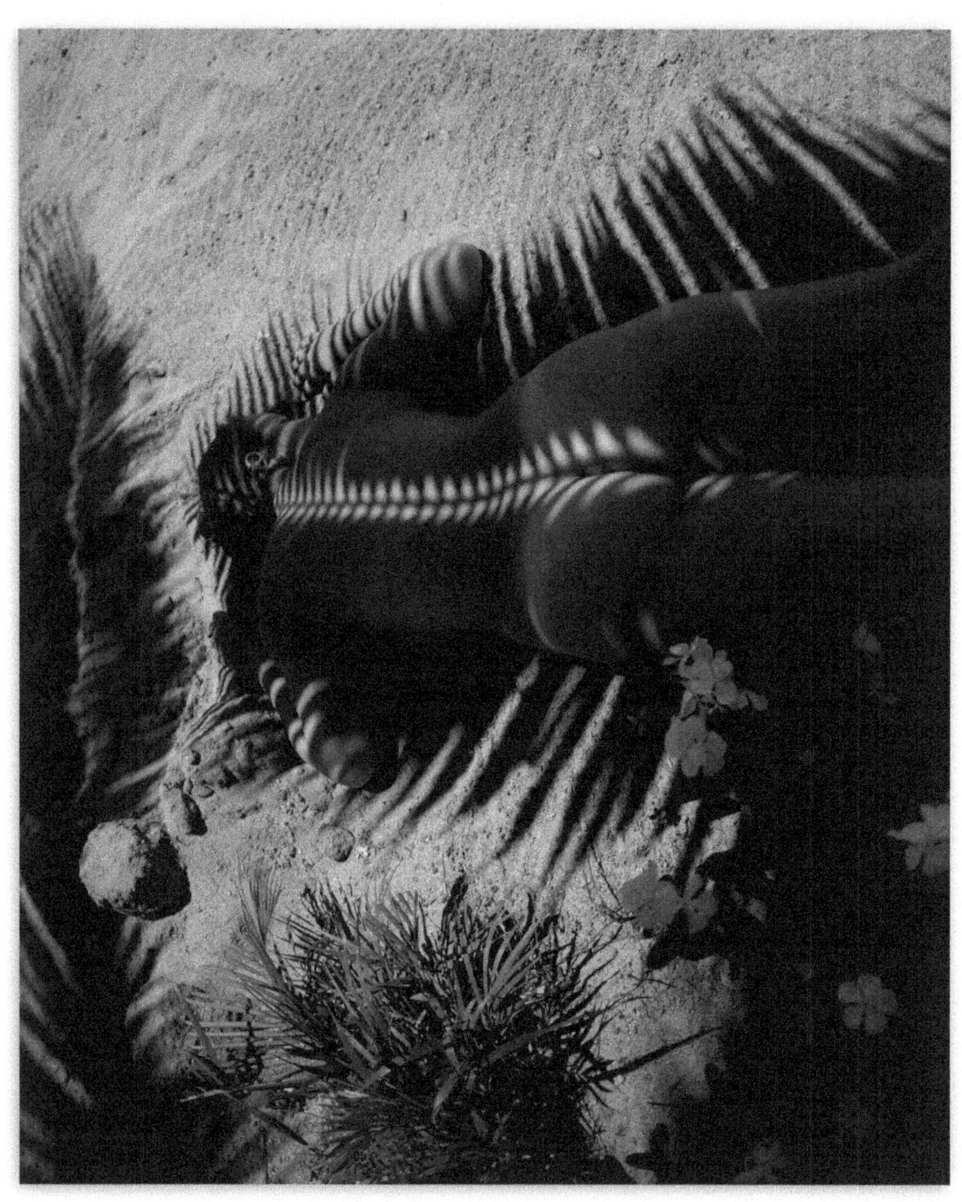

Untitled image from the project *Becoming a Specter*
Daniel W. Coburn
photograph/archival inkjet print
30x24

Untitled image from the project *Becoming a Specter*
Daniel W. Coburn
photograph/archival inkjet print
30x24

UNTITLED IMAGE FROM THE PROJECT *BECOMING A SPECTER*
Daniel W. Coburn
photograph/archival inkjet print
30x24

UNTITLED IMAGE FROM THE PROJECT *BECOMING A SPECTER*
Daniel W. Coburn
photograph/archival inkjet print
30x24

Life on the Death Panel

Mike Tuohy

Arriving thirty minutes early was not enough to beat Dr. Vladimir Volkov, exalted Chief of Neurosurgery at Qbrick Medical Center. Illuminated by the embedded monitor at his place at the head of the conference table, his face had a deathly pallor. It improved only a little as he dimmed the screen and the ambient lighting system responded to my entry. As soon as I sat down, he withdrew a foot-high statuette from his quaint brown leather briefcase and set it on the table.

"So, Dr. Gillespie, this effigy I received in the holiday gift exchange, did it originate with you?"

Fidgeting with the end of my tie, I regretted showing up early. "Actually, it's supposed to be kind of a mystery. We used to call the exchange 'Secret Santa' but somebody objected."

"Is it supposed to represent me?"

I should have known he would not recognize Professor Schizo, the mad scientist from a popular movie and video game franchise who happened to share Dr. Volkov's distinctive bald crown flanked by fountains of white hair.

"No, not at all. It's supposed to be more like an award statue, like the Oscar or the Emmy."

He stared impassively. Even after three decades in the U.S., the man openly disdained American culture and rarely acknowledged humor.

"And the electrical cord in the figure's raised hand, what does it signify?"

"It's a joke. See the card at the base?"

"Oh, yes!" He plucked the card from the statue. "Pull it, sir, prize." The man knew how to ruin a gag.

"You know. The journalism and literary award. It's a play on words."

Had I blinked, I might have missed the forced smile. "I'm sure it's very clever. Thank you."

I sensed no actual gratitude or comprehension on his part. It may have helped to explain that his colleagues often referred to him as "Vlad the Plug Puller." It may have made things worse. We passed the next 20 minutes silently perusing the patient files on the docket.

Officially, we were the Resource Allocation Committee at Qbrick Medical Center. Our weekly meetings primarily dealt with equipment procurement, pharmaceutical suppliers, staffing and other boring matters that keep a hospital running and solvent. Occasionally, we were called upon to take on weightier issues.

Over the twenty years since its enactment, the Affordable Care Act underwent many transformations. The intervening election cycles yielded ever more unfunded promises of coverage while technological advances created public demand for ever more expensive treatments. Being the nation's premier center for nanorobotic treatments, Qbrick Medical had an unlimited demand for its services but a limited capacity to deliver them. The insurance industry had a very limited desire to pay for the pricey procedures, which often exceeded half a million dollars. This resulted in a form of triage, the rules of which Congress left to individual states. After some controversial decisions and renewed outcry against government "death panels," cowardly legislatures soon assigned the process to hospital boards.

Dr. Janet Spinoza arrived five minutes late, as usual. I tried to offset Dr. Volkov's grim stare with a welcoming smile. Being the only one in the room with Dr. Volkov was excruciating.

"Janet! How are things in pediatrics?"

Janet returned my smile tenfold. She had a soft round face with dimples and a mouth that projected good will and happiness. "Oh, you know, Jeff. Whiny.

Smelly. Infinitely rewarding."

I was glad to hear her use my first name. It was our shared protest against the air of formality that dominated these proceedings.

Janet dipped her head to Vladimir. "Dr. Volkov."

The man only blinked in response. He had little tolerance for tardiness. He evinced little respect for her compassion and only a little more for my sense of ethics. Dr. Volkov was the cog of logic in our three-toothed gear, and I often thought he considered us impediments to the decision-making process.

Mindful of her infraction, Janet quickly set down her things and activated the screen at her seat. "So, what do we have here today?"

I loved her accent. Her mother was Jamaican, her father Cuban. Though she knew better, her grammar sometimes slipped, but even that was delightful. She provided a much-needed contrast to the funereal, Old World formality of our committee chairman.

Dr. Volkov gave his usual minimalist summary. "Two brain stem tumors and one upper spinal nerve damage. All three good candidates for nanobot treatments. We can only perform one given the time frames. The other two will have to wait and are unlikely to thrive."

Janet sucked air through her teeth. "Seven-hundred and fifty thousand for nanobot? We could do all three patients using more conventional treatments."

Dr. Volkov looked at me. Even if he and I used the same words, it was understood that Janet would be more receptive hearing them from me.

"Yeah, well, the problem, Janet, is the outcomes on all three would be compromised. The risk analyses shows a high likelihood of collateral tissue damage and infection, poor delivery of compounds and long recovery time for surgery and other methods. The scores are essentially identical."

Janet sighed. "Why does it always have to be this way?"

"It's why we're here. It's also why we are exempt from keeping minutes. The rules of the committee allow totally free discussion off the record."

"Thank God for that." She furrowed her brow. "Okay. Gun to my head. Candidate B. Eighty-two years old?" She looked at me. "Male? Female? Other?"

I turned my palms up. "You know we're not supposed to know about that."

"Oh, right. I was just thinking in terms of life expectancy."

Dr. Volkov rapped the tabletop with a pen. "That is already considered in the overall score."

Janet shook her head and pursed her lips. "I'm just thinking that one needs to be taken out of the running."

I looked to Vladimir. "Shall we vote on that?"

He nodded, elevated his nose and held his pen like a conductor's baton. "All in favor of removing Candidate B from consideration raise your right hand."

Janet and I looked at one another as we slowly raised our hands.

Dr. Volkov made a notation on a legal pad and muttered. "All in favor of keeping Candidate B under consideration raise your right hand." Janet and I watched, open-mouthed, as he raised his hand and made another notation.

I checked the time on my phone. I had a flight to Tahiti at 3 p.m. and it was nearly 10:30 in the morning. My ethical side kept me from mentioning this but my human component felt anxious. "Okay. Well, what about Candidate A? I mean, no dependents or close relatives."

Janet nodded. "I see what you mean. Candidate C has three young grandchildren. I mean, he may be older but, you know. That's family."

That triggered one of my alarms. I happened to know that Janet was having numerous family members stay at her home over the holidays. She surely wanted to get away to start preparing. Ethically, I had to put such concerns out of my mind, but we were friends. How could I do that?

The vote was unanimous. A was out. We were down to B versus C.

Janet smiled as if already smelling the aroma of jerk chicken and *lechon asado*. "Well then this is a no-brainer. C has grandbabies and B is too old. Let's vote."

We looked eagerly to Dr. Volkov, who sat with fingers steepled. Without a word he slid us each a piece of paper, printed side down. I slapped my hand over my copy. Before I could advise Janet to do the same, she read aloud. "Philanthropist Benjamin C. Putnam diagnosed with inoperable brain tumor."

Snatching the page away from her, I stood and pointed at Vladimir. "This is an egregious violation of ethical standards. This negates the sanctity and validity of our committee's mission!"

The man stared at me until it became clear he would not address me until I sat down. I sat, glancing only momentarily at Janet, who looked away, biting her lip.

Dr. Volkov addressed Janet first. "What else did you just learn about Mr. Putnam? What did you already know?"

She shrugged. "I saw that he recently donated two million dollars to this hospital. I already knew the pediatric wing was named for him."

"Quite right." He looked to me. "Same question."

"You can't live in this town without knowing the name and what he has done. It doesn't justify giving him preference for medical treatment. That's what this committee is supposed to prevent. It shouldn't just be about the patient's wealth."

Dr. Volkov nodded. "I appreciate your high moral standard, Jeff."

“I prefer ‘ethical’ and to you it’s ‘Dr. Gillespie.’”

He gave me that split-second smile. “Very well, Dr. Gillespie, but I should tell you I was involved in Mr. Putnam’s initial diagnosis. However, I was not directly informed of his identity for the purposes of this meeting. I just happened to know enough of his personal details to glean his identity from what is normally provided.”

“Then you should have recused yourself from this decision. Found a substitute.”

Vladimir leaned back in his chair. “There was no time. I only realized the likely identity this morning and, as you know, the committee rules require a minimum three-person quorum. Nobody wants this task. I certainly don’t, but it must be done in a timely manner.”

Janet waved a finger in the air. “Just a second, now. This Benjamin Putnam, billionaire, gives us a couple of million every year or so. Now, I’m just putting this out there as something to think about. How much you think he’s going to leave us when he dies? Hundred million? Two hundred million?”

Aghast, I stood up and turned to her. “Dr. Spinoza! Are you advocating we kill the goose?”

Janet looked momentarily confused then bade me to sit back down.

“I wouldn’t put it that way, but, if we had, say, a hundred million dollars right now we could treat all three of these patients with the best possible outcome without all this grief. Besides, you told me yourself, each time we use this nanobot technology, the process gets better and cheaper. Having that money now will bring the future sooner.”

“But that is just as fundamentally wrong a reason as favoring him because he’s rich!”

Janet shrugged. “Dr. Volkov hasn’t exactly told us which one is Mr. Putnam.

Has he?"

Her tone and expression made it clear that no words could change her mind. She knew as well as I did that Candidate B was the old rich man.

Dr. Volkov cleared his throat. "I propose a vote." He looked from me to Janet. "There being no objections, all in favor of eliminating Candidate B from consideration, raise your right hand."

Janet avoided my gaze as she slowly raised her hand. I kept staring at her as I raised mine. I wanted her to know how much I resented the quandary she put me in. Her shocked expression made me turn to see Dr. Volkov displaying an upright palm.

He smiled a full second or more. "Then it is unanimous. Enjoy your holiday."

"What the hell, Volkov?"

He gestured to Janet. "She made a very compelling argument."

Seizing his pen, I quickly wrote on the blank side of the paper in front of me and slid it to him. "My resignation."

Janet nudged me. "Good move, but I think we just voted ourselves unnecessary for the next few years."

My colleagues looked at me as if expecting a pithy parting comment. The best I could do was state one thing I still knew to be true. "I have a plane to catch."

Orange Foam

Richard King Perkins II

If possible,
I'd love you strangely;

a different body with different parts

inducing trace throbs of response
more luscious

than anything either of us
has ever known before.

Beneath a triangle of sun

in the orange foam of an ocean
never possible

in any previous
world of castles and useless skin,

my gills will flutter and sing.

Beauty of Life
Yue Li
oil on canvas
24x36

Seize the Time
Yue Li
charcoal
18x24

Actions Speak Louder than Words
Yue Li
pencil
18x24

Storing the Dark

KB Ballentine

A fist of starlight fractures clouds
fastened on the horizon,
sheets forgotten on the line
when I pursued the ambulance from the house.
Hydrangeas fuss and whisper,
doves grieving in their gloom,
crust of moon in a leftover sky.

Mom's visit now a six-month sojourn,
the garden grass, bent and worn,
reveals the trail she paces every morning.
Gait and gaze wandering, she strokes the chicory, the clematis.
Mama, just for a moment we're happy.

Windows still dark, I bundle the clothes,
begin to smooth and fold.
Like her mother used to do in the gray dawn,
before day shifted into color, into tune.
Sprigs of lavender tucked into creases,
she bridged time and sorrow
with piles traded for stacks small enough
to set on a shelf, close the door, and walk away.

Madelyn Without the Moonlight

Lisa Marie Brodsky

She was planned in girlhood diary notes,
written in long loops
and curly i's.

As a woman, I loved men
who always promised something
I'd eventually lose.

But when one man said, *love,*
I thought it time
to give her a name.

Madelyn is a shadow
who will never see light
or the sun that would've browned her face.

Like the unrolling of crayon ribbons,
her imprint curls off the table
and falls in scraps at my feet.

There's a death the *maybe* brings,
like a noose hooking the curly 'i'
and dropping it

suddenly. These promises expire
and go the way of all discarded vows—

toward the dark that rivals

the moon's blinking tease of life,
its eclipse, the baby's final turn
away in the womb.

Rush Hour
Michael Young
acrylic
46x30

Trip to the Funny Farm
Michael Young
acrylic
48x36

Corner Sales
Michael Young
acrylic
36x24

Up, Up, and Away
Michael Young
acrylic
28x34

You're Going To Be OK

R.S. Wynn

I used to cut in the shower. When I finished gently shaving hair from ankle to thigh, I pressed the razor's warm metal blade down into my leg and slowly carved out thick petals of skin. For a breath there wasn't any blood, just water gracing the exposed flesh and a pure white sting as deeper layers of my body were washed clean. Then the laceration turned blotchy, variegated as a rose. Finally, blood flowed, snaking around my kneecaps, dripping off the precipice of my calves. Sometimes I'd lean forward to catch the blood in the cup of my palm and I'd examine the pooling red, studious as a jeweler peering through her glass.

I was eleven years old when I started this gory ritual. Once out of the shower, I was careful not to get blood anywhere. I patted the raw skin on my legs dry with toilet paper. Fibers got stuck and I delicately plucked the torn paper from my wounds with my fingernails—if I stained a towel, though, I risked being discovered by my parents. I treated the cuts with Betadine, which dyed my skin crocus yellow, and then tenderly wrapped my legs in bandages. When I went to bed at night, I'd unwrap them to feel the cool, dry air whisper across my skin. By the next morning the pain lessened, and in a few days a layer of crisp, tissue-paper cells formed across the wounds, protecting me anew. My purpose wasn't to hurt myself. The blade unearthed the pervasive, shapeless ache I felt and gave it a locus, a form. Made it comprehensible. But what I craved most was measurable recovery: proof that I could heal.

In order to truly heal I thought, or maybe I'd been told, I had to identify the source of my inner turmoil. I focused in on my misery, tried to pinpoint where in my short and ordinary life it had come from. My parents loved me, though they'd made mistakes, and I'd had a happy childhood. In sixth grade, when I started cutting, I had clear skin and good teeth. I had a solid group of friends. My hips were rounding out and my stomach was no longer svelte as a child's. My breasts ached as they grew. More than one boy had a crush on me. Despite all this, I felt I was different from my peers, and often alone. I was alone when I dug into myself for answers. All I unearthed was blood.

I cut my legs because they were easier to conceal than my arms or wrists. Of all the self-harming rituals I engaged in as a teenager—smoking, drinking, shoplifting—I think my parents would have found cutting the most disturbing, but the only adult who saw the cuts on my legs was my sixth-grade gym teacher. I forgot to bring gym pants one day and she loaned me an extra pair of shorts she kept handy in her office for just such an occasion. I didn't know how to refuse, so I put the shorts on and emerged from the locker room hopeful that maybe no one would notice the intricate patchwork of scars on my legs and seeping bandages that covered new wounds.

When the gym teacher saw me, she dropped the whistle she was about to blow and it bounced against her hard chest on a lariat. "What happened to your legs?" she gasped, stopping me with her hand on my shoulder.

"I—I had to turn off an outside light last night," I said. "It was dark, and I walked through some rose bushes."

I'd had little cause to lie in my life and I still lied artlessly, like a child. It didn't look like the gym teacher believed me—who would have?—but what could she do? I never forgot my gym pants again, and she never again spoke about what she'd seen.

In seventh grade—I was twelve then, and had been cutting for a year—I was called out of class one day and directed to the guidance counselor's office. She asked me the usual questions, or at least what I imagined usual questions were based on therapists I'd seen on TV. *How would you describe your mood?* Fine—she stared at me expectantly—sad sometimes, I guess. *What makes you feel sad?* I dunno. *Does anyone hurt you?* I don't think so. No?

As I sat in her office, I remember being aware that she too was digging for a source. If I was sad, there must be a reason. If I was in pain, there must be a wound. How could I tell her that *I* was the only one who hurt me? How could she understand it was what I felt I needed?

Adults tend to downplay the emotional distress of children—I do it now too. I remember when my youngest step-daughter was nine I scolded her at a birthday party when she pulled the candles out of her friend's birthday cake and licked the frosting off them. I wasn't angry. I didn't yell. But I grabbed her hand as she reached for another candle and said, "It's not your birthday and that's not your cake. That's not OK." She ran off, tears bright in her eyes, her cheeks round and red as garnet. I shrugged off her tantrum—I was right about the cake after all—but when I found her sulking and asked her to rejoin the party she said she was too sad and angry, an emotional brew I now recognize as shame. "It's just cake," I offered as consolation. "It's not the end of the world."

I wonder now if the pain she experienced then was less intense—because she was nine and the incident involved cake—than the pain I've felt as an adult over the death of a loved one or a failed marriage? Or maybe, could that pain be greater *because* she was only nine and for a nine-year-old so much of the world is inscrutable and daunting? W. B. Yeats wrote that the suffering of children is worse than the suffering of adults, "because we can see the end of our trouble and they can never see any end."

*

A few weeks after seeing the school counselor, I suddenly stopped cutting. I was worried that teachers might be talking about me, or that friends, maybe, had reported me. I'd like to say I found healthier outlets for my emotions, but really paranoia had spilled over into my self-soothing and cutting no longer offered any release.

In the shower before school one morning, I pressed the hot, steel blade into my leg, but when I started to peel back my skin, my mother knocked loudly on the bathroom door. The school bus would be there soon, she said, I had to hurry. I wondered what she would think if she could see me cutting, so near to her, hidden only by a door. Would she be disgusted? Would she faint or cry at the sight of her daughter's ravaged skin? Would she blame herself? Water hammered into the new incision and blood dripped onto the shower floor but no calm followed in its wake. Just a hollow sting, and shame.

In some cultures, scarification is a rite of passage. In the Sepik region of Papua New Guinea, boys around eleven years old are initiated by elders who slice their backs with bamboo, patterning the scars to look like the skin of a crocodile. Girls in parts of Ethiopia and Sudan are scarred across their faces, stomachs, and chests starting as young as ten years old, marking major life events from puberty, to marriage, to the birth of their children. But in those cultures, cutting is communal, an open acknowledgement of the difficult road children must navigate to reach adulthood. Here, we like to imagine that our children feel no pain—no *real* pain.

I'm in my thirties now and like many adults I have forgotten the language of the eleven-year-old psyche. I have little tolerance for pain, my own or the pain of others. I'm a vegetarian. I recycle. I like yin yoga. I love my three step-daughters and I cry when we watch movies together, even animated films. I'm careful with myself. I don't like to get so much as a paper cut on my finger. Even the angriest of my old scars is gone, as if everything can be made new.

In June, my youngest step-daughter will turn eleven, the age I was when I started cutting. Sometimes she cries and doesn't know why. Large, heavy tears stream down her face, clinging to the curve of her cheek like moonstone. She wipes them away with the back of her hand and in that innocent gesture she looks five years old again. She could always explain why she was upset when she was five. Because she couldn't have ice cream for breakfast. Because she'd lost a game and she wanted her friend to lose. Because she feared her beloved stuffed dragon might drown in the washing machine. Her pain was explicit and the cause crystalline. Such is the wisdom of very young children.

What would have been an easy cry a year ago is now overburdened. Shocked by the power of her emotions and frustrated by her inability to grasp their origin, she flies into a frenzy. I wish I could remember something that helped me when I was her age, something that didn't involve explaining one pain with another. My husband, who already raised his two older daughters through their teenage years, says that all I need to tell her is that I love her, she's good, and she's going to be OK. He says it doesn't matter what she does, just repeat those words like a mantra: *I love you. You're good. You're going to be OK.*

But some nights she takes long showers, singing radio anthems of mean girls and cheating men, which she belts out joyfully because the melodies are catchy and the lyrics are still foreign to her experience. She often rewrites the words for fun, throwing in a couple extra "oh yeahs" and "uh huh, babys" for good measure. Pearls of soap and water burst against the shower curtain as she stomps and claps her hands, almost in rhythm. On the other side of the closed door I listen, waiting to hear if her feet stop moving, if her song falls silent.

That Time We First Smoked Pot

Susana H. Case

or what we thought was pot
but was oregano or similar,
the four of us sat, silent,
parked on a dark side street
off Queens Boulevard, waiting
for something to happen,

listening to Chuck Berry
on the Chevy radio, *Nadine,*
No Particular Place To Go.

We watched one another
for signs that maybe something
was happening to someone else,
watched the windows fogging.

Waited. So much of the teen
years were like that: We waited,
nothing nothing nothing happened.

Except, everything was happening.
We just didn't know it, used
our fingers to write our names
in the condensation
and waited some more.

News of a Friend's Passing

Kathy O'Fallon

Think that someone may bring
a bear to your door. —Robert Bly

I was sitting at my computer working
on something like this when I felt the presence
of otherworldliness—why not, all things
a dream—slowly turned my head,
caught the shimmer of mahogany—
magnificent Ursidae! Huge sweetness
of truth, power of introspection, food
of the mystery. His snout
pointed, as if calling me to the future.
Who are you to me? I longed to touch
his radiance but kept my hands
on the keys—wasn't it for him to give,
or take me? So I breathed as I'd learned
at the meditation retreat, from the nose—
breath in, breath out—his own feathering
my neck, his tongue a baptism,
his head nestling in my crook.
No raven swooping in, leaving nothing
but grief, Dick chose the bear
of the long winter sleep, the one
who wakes to the shadow of its body.

Untitled

Kathy O'Fallon

My bones a weather report,
I know there's no need for experts, for cyberspace,
that the body can tell me everything about myself—

this encyclopedic world an immaculate nakedness.
So many flowers to name, I can't resist,
yet every glimpse invites the virgin.

So more and more I'm finding
it's enough that these moments exist,
that words don't mean what I think,

that when I reach deeply enough,
the well is a space of infinity.
We are so sweet on description,

and I know it's a kind of praise
to feel the way the tongue folds
around words like "calendula,"

to wonder at the science of a flower
made especially to heal injury,
and yet, as I forget more words

with every advancing year,
I no longer grieve.
My well empties, leaves only fragrance.

Mama's Recipe for Mujaddara

Shahé Mankerian

Pour bulgur in the cracked demitasse
and set it on the window ledge;
little sunlight clears the pantry moth.

Avoid the lentil in the burlap sack;
it's made in Turkey and full of pebbles.
I hid the Ziyad Brothers in the canister;

they import their grains from Aleppo.
Be frugal. Use your palm for measure.
"This is the last batch," said Mahmood

at the grocery store. "Syria is burning."
The colander is above the refrigerator.
It's your father's green helmet from the army;

he drilled holes in it last summer.
It works perfectly for rinsing. Don't tell
Father we're using the pressure cooker

for mujaddara. He won't eat it. Listen,
cook it over a low heat on the left burner
before he gets home from the bakery.

Drizzle extra virgin olive oil in the saucepan.
Excuse the dents, rust, the spatula scratches.
Chop a head of yellow onion, simmer it

in the pan. When it's caramelized,
it must match the color of Mademoiselle
Bshara's dyed hair. Poor girl went gray

when she lost her fiancé at the massacre
of Tel al-Zaatar. Before you set the dishes,
spread the newspaper like a tablecloth.

Father doesn't like to talk when eating.

If We Just Lollygag Around Here a Bit Longer

Deborah Bacharach

The bananas will strike up the band,
start the march through main street.
Yup, we have a permit.

The glue refuses to join.
That's her prerogative.
That's her whispering
sweet nothings to the avocado.

The grapefruit is not an avocado.
But you were not stunned to learn that.
You have been on the threshold,
refused (but politely) to cross in.

If I get the Colossus of Rhodes,
I can win all the wars and build a university.
I'll put dormers over the back alleys,
so you can hear the late night guitars.

Your daughter carries
a murmuration of worries—
the house burnt down, the key lost, the brother
not loved enough.

If your dreams are peripatetic,
as they so often are, ask
Marguerite to hug you.
In her bright green coat, she will hug you.

MMS: Odin
Barbara Waterman-Peters
oil on canvas
20x20

MWS: The Event Planners
Barbara Waterman-Peters
oil on canvas
36x24

The Walnut Concertos

Rick Forbess

The concertos began when Doodie first encountered Thomas a month earlier. She was walking across the quadrangle after leaving social skills class, and he was walking in the opposite direction straight toward her, talking to himself. The first few bars of Bach's Concerto in A major filled her ears when they passed and then ended after a few more steps. Doodie thought she may have been hallucinating, but when she turned and caught up with him, she heard the concerto again. She stopped, and Thomas walked on. Doodie went straight to her room, got in bed, and pulled the covers over her head. "I'm Doodie Schwartz. I'm a cello player," she whispered to herself. "I'm Doodie Schwartz. I'm a murderer," she countered. She debated with herself for some time like this, stopping after each declaration to reflect. The slight possibility that the cello player Doodie could be reborn, she decided, was a miracle. She wondered if Thomas was an angel, a real angel, not another resident like it seemed. She thought it must be true, but knew not to tell anyone. They would think she was still insane.

Several times a week, in the rec room with the TV on in the background or alone in the hallway late at night, Doodie listened to Thomas speak and waited for the music to begin. His words hovered before floating upward through the ceiling and drifting over the countryside, as the melody filled the space around them. The topic might have been the distance of the earth from the nearest non-sun star, or the multi-verse theory, or the joys of composting, or, lately, black walnut trees. Thomas knew a great deal about nearly everything, and it seemed to Doodie that he wanted to tell her about all of it. The music would start when he spoke, and the sadness, fear, and anger that lurked in her heart shrunk to the size of a pea. Thomas was in his own space, a place he seemed comfortable with and that made it possible for him to be at ease with others. He was not fearful nor to be feared, wounded nor angry, and the music Doodie heard when he spoke was a powerful tonic. Neither the medication, nor the cheerleading to recover, nor the field trips to the mall were a match for the elixir that was Thomas.

*

It was unclear to Doodie at times whether Thomas had appeared out of thin air, or if she just hadn't noticed that he was there the whole time. Once she asked him this question point blank when they were in the cafeteria serving line. One moment she was alone, and the next Thomas was standing behind her holding his empty tray.

He smiled at the question, and said, "What do you think?"

"I don't know, that's why I asked," she replied. "You seem like a person who can do whatever you want to, Thomas, and it's not because you're so tall."

Thomas glanced around the large room. "Over there," he gestured with a nod, "let's take that table next to the window. We can soak up some photons. Know what photons are? Elementary particles that also have the properties of a wave. You gotta know your quantum mechanics to really get it, and that's a tall order for any person."

They sat together at the table, Thomas talking and Doodie waiting for the music as she ate. Her slice of pizza was half eaten when she heard a familiar opening bar from a piece she could not quite name at first, but then, "That's Vivaldi," she said. "Concerto for Violin and Cello in B-flat major."

"You're one of a kind, Doodie," Thomas said.

*

A week after Doodie's first encounter with Thomas, she and he stood at the end of the hallway hidden in shadows from the nurses' station. It was late and she wasn't able to sleep.

"*Juglans nigra,*" Thomas spoke softly, almost in a whisper, "common name, eastern black walnut; aka money tree." Right away his words grew fainter and were barely audible to Doodie under the lilting melody.

"Both the wood and the nuts are valuable," Thomas continued, "and on top of that, you can boil the sap to make syrup, which would be a nice little novelty item. They're hardy and easy to grow too. Just plant a couple hundred, tend to them for twenty years or so, and you're a millionaire. That's pretty much all there is to it. The return on investment averages around 14% a year. Call it the walnut IRA."

As the last notes faded, Doodie hugged Thomas, and it was not something fleeting and awkward. She wrapped both arms tightly around him with her head buried in his chest, and held on. Thomas stood with his arms to his sides, unmoving for an uncomfortably long few seconds before gently resting the side of his face on the top of Doodie's head and speaking, still in a near whisper. "Ever heard of Valles Marineris, second largest canyon in the solar system? It's up on Mars, and it's twenty-five hundred miles long, a hundred and twenty miles wide, as deep as Mount Everest is high."

Doodie did not answer, but Thomas responded as if she had. "Well, we got the Great Rift right here on Earth, and it's bigger, and people walk out of it all the time, so you just may do the same."

*

Over the course of a few days Doodie began to sleep better and smile more often, follow the ward rules, participate in activities, and even compliment staff on their appearance. The changes were surprising, and when the expected return of the surly, withdrawn, noncompliant Doodie didn't happen, a measure of self-congratulatory optimism emerged among the treatment team members. During the next case review, their observations and perspectives about reasons and implications were reported, and the possibility of her discharge was discussed for the first time. Dr. Bobo listened, nodding his head and smiling until they finished, and then reminded the team that Doodie would have to display an extended period of stability before discharge could be considered. He expressed concern that she may be experiencing a "manic swing that will lead to a hard landing when it ends."

Dr. Bobo was Doodie's psychiatrist. Once a month or so they met in his office for five or ten minutes, and he asked her a few questions that never varied in content or order. Her answers were the same each time, "No," "Yes," "Sort of," "I guess so," "Not yet," and "No." Dr. Bobo smiled the whole time in a way that

Doodie thought was inappropriate for the situational context and made her feel uncomfortable. "Inappropriate affect," she thought. In their first meeting, he asked her a question that she'd been answering for years. "What does the saying 'People who live in glass houses should not throw stones' mean?" Doodie thought it was the lamest question ever. The answer was obvious, "They would ruin their house," but because she thought it was an insulting question to ask someone you'd just met, she said, "That's a stupid question. I won't answer it." Dr. Bobo kept smiling and bent his head to the laptop keyboard to enter her answer. "Keep taking your meds," he always said when they parted.

*

The day after her case review Doodie arrived on time for the Resident Unit Meeting without prompts from the staff. When the routine question "Does anyone have anything you want to share?" was asked, she raised her hand. The staff facilitator and the few residents who were paying attention turned to Doodie, surprised by her unprecedented behavior.

"I want to share that I'll be leaving Skyhaven before long. I'll miss some of you. I really will, but it's time for me." One resident applauded vigorously while another asked, "When do you get out of this nuthouse?"

Before Doodie could respond, the facilitator broke in. "A lot of planning and preparation has to go on before someone is discharged, and also the judge would have to give the green light. Have you given any thought to what you'd do, where you'd live, any of that?"

"Of course I have," Doodie replied. "I'm going to have an eastern black walnut orchard." As soon as she uttered the sentence, she heard the opening notes of a concerto, but the music faded in absence of Thomas speaking.

News of Doodie's plan traveled fast among the staff, and when it reached Dr. Bobo, he arranged an evaluation session with her the next day. In addition to the usual questions about hearing voices, taking her medication, whether she was getting along with staff and residents, etc., he probed to learn more about the reasons for the change in her mood lately and about what she had shared in Resident's Council. He was concerned, he explained to her. "Some residents get it in their head to be discharged before they are ready, and when I tell them this, they become angry or depressed. I hope you won't have that reaction, Doodie, but you aren't ready now. I will have to convince the judge that you can live in the community with proper treatment and support and no longer be a risk to society. That is what I want to do, but I cannot do it now. Do you agree?"

"You can't or you won't?" she asked.

Ignoring the question, he said, "Now, Doodie, I understand it is an orchard, one with nuts, that you plan to own when you leave here, but you have no orchard with nuts, you have no money to buy the orchard, do you?" She did not respond, so he continued, "My grandparents immigrated to California from the Philippines in 1920's, and when my father was a teenager he worked alongside them harvesting grapes. It was such hard, hard work, with very little pay. My grandparents and father were so worn out and so desperate that they returned to their homeland where my father met my mother. I know that keeping an orchard of nuts is something you cannot do. Also, it was a very serious crime you committed. You understand this. You have told me that you do."

Doodie's memory of driving the car into the lake was always close by except when she heard the concertos. She didn't clearly recall the details of that day nor of the several days before, but she remembered the voices commanding her and the ice-cold water flooding the interior of the car. She remembered rolling the window down and being surprised that the water level was no deeper than the top of the front door. She remembered standing on the shore and her shock at seeing Sarah Sue's long black hair floating on the top of the water in the back seat just a few feet away. She remembered the judge saying "Not guilty by reason of insanity." She remembered that she wasn't allowed to attend her sister's funeral.

*

Thomas had told her that every patient (they were called "residents" at this place) had a legal right to read his or her chart, and Doodie wanted to judge where she stood in Dr. Bobo's eyes, so she made a request to read his most recent progress assessment. Dr. Bobo felt that Doodie's "therapeutic gain" had been "minimal" since her admission to the hospital two years ago. He wrote that her thinking was often "grandiose," and that there was "a consistent delusional element to her cognitive process." She didn't totally understand all the terms, but knew it was not a favorable report. "What does that dodo, Bobo, know?" she wondered.

After reading the report, she went back to her room, under the covers to sort it all out. "Dr. Bobo would change his mind if he knew how well I am," she whispered to herself, "if he knew about Thomas and the music." He had always said that if she had a really important reason, he could speak to her between their scheduled sessions, so the next morning, rather than go to horticulture therapy, she waited for Dr. Bobo under a tree next to the parking lot and asked for a meeting as they walked side by side from his car toward his office. He agreed to see her that afternoon and said that he would pass the word on to the ward staff.

Doodie thanked him and when he closed the office door, she turned to find Thomas standing there in front of her. The morning sun was streaming in from a high window almost directly behind him, casting a sheet of light that glowed around his silhouetted outline.

"Thomas! Where did you come from?" Doodie asked.

"It's true that it takes effort and persistence to grow, harvest, and shell eastern black walnuts, but they are the most delicious of all walnuts," Thomas said, disregarding the question.

"That's Bach, again, Cello Suite Number 1 in G," Doodie said, closing her eyes and leaning back on the corridor wall. Thomas was nowhere to be seen when the music ended.

*

The meeting with Dr. Bobo began awkwardly for Doodie. She didn't know how to start and was having second thoughts about whether it would be helpful to disclose the miracle or not.

"What did you want to discuss, Doodie?" Dr. Bobo asked.

"I don't know if it's a discussion or not, more like I've been thinking of telling you something," Doodie replied.

"Okay, anything you'd like."

"Well, it's kind of hard to explain it."

"Yes, I understand. Some things are difficult to bring up but also necessary, for the better," he said. "Is this the case for you now?"

Doodie held a steady gaze and put both hands over her mouth until she could no longer hold back. Hardly taking a breath, her words gushed out in a torrent. "Thomas is a resident here. I think he may be my guardian angel, a real angel. When he speaks, I hear concertos, and that's why I've been in such a good mood. He knows all about eastern black walnuts and a whole lot more. I think he wants me to own an eastern black walnut orchard, and he'll be there to help. Please don't hold any of this against me or think I'm crazy."

Dr. Bobo leaned back in his chair and then forward to rest his elbows on the desk with his hands clasped. "So, you believe there is an angel who will help you with the orchard of walnuts. I see. Now tell me, Doodie, who is this Thomas?"

Staring at her feet, Doodie answered softly. "He's a resident, but I don't know what unit he's on. It doesn't matter. He can show up wherever he wants to."

"Doodie, there are 53 residents living in our forensic units, and I know half of them personally. I'm aware of the other half, even though I'm not their psychiatrist. There is no Thomas among them. I'm sure of this, and none of the residents here is an angel," Dr. Bobo said.

"I knew you wouldn't believe me. You think I'm crazy," Doodie said.

"That is an unkind and unprofessional term. You have a mental illness. There should be no shame about that, but this illness makes you see and hear angels. They are not real," Dr. Bobo said as he leaned to his left to pick up his pen which had rolled off the desk. When he straightened and turned to Doodie, a rather tall man was standing next to the chair where Doodie sat.

"Billions of years from now the universe will be a cold and lonely place because all the galaxies will have traveled so far apart as the universe and time itself expands," Thomas said.

"I'm sorry, you're in the wrong office. Where are you going? Can I give you directions?" he asked Thomas and discreetly reached for his phone to dial security.

Doodie was lost to it all, floating on the notes of Schumann's Concerto for Cello and Orchestra in A minor, but Dr. Bobo turned his attention to Thomas, who was still talking about the expanding universe. "You must leave now. I'm this woman's psychiatrist, and this is a confidential session."

Thomas switched topics and continued talking while Doodie rested comfortably in her chair with her eyes closed, humming a melody. "In the 1930s Filipino immigrants worked the grape orchards of California and were often brought in as strike breakers, to take jobs from Mexicans and poor whites. They were all desperate people just trying to feed and shelter their families."

Dr. Bobo closed his eyes, and his chin sunk to his chest. "What is that lovely melody?" he asked.

Naili Teddy Bear
Anna Bevitt
ink and graphite
5.5x8.5

CONTRIBUTORS

Deborah Bacharach is the author of *After I Stop Lying* (Cherry Grove Collections, 2015). A two-time nominee for the Pushcart Prize, her work has appeared in *The Antigonish Review, Blue Mesa Review, Calyx,* and *Dunes,* among many others. Find out more about her at DeborahBacharach.com

KB Ballentine's fifth collection of poems, *Almost Everything, Almost Nothing,* was recently released by Middle Creek Publishing. Her work also appears in *In God's Hand* (2017), *River of Earth and Sky: Poems for the Twenty-first Century* (2015), *Southern Poetry Anthology, Volume VI: Tennessee* (2013), and *Southern Light: Twelve Contemporary Southern Poets* (2011).

Anna Bevitt is a senior in high school who has taken art classes every semester. While her artistic style is reminiscent of manga and anime, she strives to create things that are truly original. She retains a wide cast of unique characters and locations in her head and attempts to tell their stories on paper through both visual art and creative writing.

Lisa Marie Brodsky is the author of the poetry collections *We Nod Our Dark Heads* (Parallel Press, 2008) and *Motherlung* (Salmon Poetry, 2014), which received an Outstanding Achievement Award from the Wisconsin Library Association. Brodsky teaches workshops on emotional healing through creative writing.

James Cagney is a poet and writer from Oakland, California. He has appeared as a featured poet and artist at venues in Sacramento, San Francisco, Vancouver, Chicago, and Mumbai. Visit his blog at https://thedirtyrat.blog/

Susana H. Case is the author of five books of poetry, most recently *Drugstore Blue,* from Five Oaks Press, and *4 Rms w Vu,* from Mayapple Press, as well as four chapbooks. She is a professor and program coordinator at the New York Institute of Technology in New York City.

Daniel W. Coburn's work investigates the family photo album as one component of a visual infrastructure that reinforces the flawed ideology of the American Dream. His photo-based works have been published widely and have been the subject of major national and international exhibitions. He is the recipient of a 2017 John Simon Guggenheim Memorial Fellowship. He currently serves as assistant professor of photography at the University of Kansas.

Roberta P. Feins received her M.F.A. in poetry from New England College. Her poems have been published in *Five AM, Antioch Review, The Cortland Review,* and *The Gettysburg Review,* among others. She has published two chapbooks: *Something Like a River* (Moon Path Press, 2013) and *Herald* (Autumn House Press, 2017).

Harvey Flowers is a ceramic artist and street photographer from Topeka, Kansas. He is currently pursuing a degree in fine arts with an emphasis in ceramics and sculpture at Washburn University.

Rick Forbess lives in Maine with his wife of 47 years and his 96-year-old mother-in-law. (It works.) He was born and educated in Texas, from which he fled in 1980. His career, from which he is semi-retired, has been in the mental health field.

Clemonce Heard is a native of New Orleans. He graduated from Northwestern State University in Natchitoches, Louisiana where he received his B.F.A. in graphic communications and minored in culinary arts. He is currently a candidate for Oklahoma State University's M.F.A. in poetry.

Dawn Hogue, a Wisconsin writer, is the winner of the 2017 Hal Prize for Poetry. Her poetry has also appeared in *Stoneboat Literary Journal, Making it Speak: Artists and Writers in Cahoots*, and *Intersections: Art and Poetry. A Hollow Bone*, her debut novel from Water's Edge Press, was released June 2017.

Jan LaPerle lives in east Tennessee with her husband, Clay Matthews, and daughter, Winnie. She has published a book of poetry, *It Would Be Quiet* (Prime Mincer Press, 2013), an e-chap of flash fiction, *Hush* (Sundress Publications, 2012), a story in verse, *A Pretty Place to Mourn* (BlazeVOX, 2014), and several other stories and poems. In 2014 she won an individual artist grant from the Tennessee Arts Commission.

Yue Li was born into a family of artists in Sichuan Province, China, in 1998. She gets lots of inspiration from the human body, which she believes can express the strongest feelings and give people inspiration. She is an art student at Washburn University.

Shahé Mankerian is the principal of St. Gregory Hovsepian School in Pasadena, California and the co-director of the L.A. Writing Project. He is the recipient of the Los Angeles Music Center's BRAVO Award, which recognizes teachers for innovation in arts education. In 2017, Shahé received the Editors' Prize from *MARY: A Journal of New Writing*.

Justin Marable has created art professionally for 14 years and currently resides in Lawrence, Kansas with his wife and three daughters. From his home and East Lawrence studio, he creates in various styles and media. His concepts constantly evolve and have transformed into numerous bodies of work and exhibitions throughout his career.

Ellen Birkett Morris's fiction has appeared in *Shenandoah, Antioch Review, Notre Dame Review, South Carolina Review*, and *Santa Fe Literary Review*, among other journals. She is the 2015 winner of the Bevel Summers Prize for her story "May Apples." Her story "Like I Miss Being a Ballerina" was selected as an honorable mention in the Glimmer Train Press Family Matters short story competition.

Kathy O'Fallon's poems and short stories have been published in dozens of literary journals, magazines, and anthologies. She is a psychologist living in Fallbrook, California, avocado capital of the world.

Jim O'Loughlin is the author of the flash fiction collection *Dean Dean Dean Dean* (Twelve Winters Press) and the coordinator of the Final Thursday Reading Series in Cedar Falls, Iowa. He teaches English at the University of Northern Iowa.

Richard King Perkins II is a state-sponsored advocate for residents in long-term care facilities. He lives in Crystal Lake, Illinois, with his wife, Vickie, and daughter, Sage. He is a three-time Pushcart, Best of the Net, and Best of the Web nominee whose work has appeared in more than 1,000 publications.

David Lee Quick grew up in Wichita, Kansas and attended Friends University. In 1967 he moved to Philadelphia, served as artist-in-residence at the University of Pennsylvania, and taught in Quaker private schools. He served on the National Ethics Committee of Artists Equity and lobbied Congress regarding issues affecting artists. Returning to Kansas in 1991, he taught art history at Wichita State University and organized the first major Kansas Latina-Latino art exhibition. He continues to advocate for the arts while working on his art and photography in Wichita.

Tyler Quintin received his B.F.A. in studio arts from Washburn University in 2016. He was a recipient of the Barbara L. Buzick scholarship, a four-year, full-tuition scholarship. Since graduating, he has worked as the assistant gallery director at SouthWind Art Gallery in Topeka, Kansas, and is a NOTO Arts Place artist-in-residence. Currently, he is employed at Washburn's Mulvane Art Museum, assisting with the installation of the new Rita Blitt Gallery. His work has been exhibited nationally and internationally and is represented in the permanent collection of the Mulvane.

Robert Rickelman was born in Chicago. He earned his B.A. in Spanish at the University of Arizona, which is where he was introduced to, and deeply affected by, the Latin American genre of Magical Realism. He tries to explore this genre in most of his writing.

Cara Rodriguez is an English instructor at Casper College. Her work draws from day-to-day life, ordinary process, and relationship to the world. She won the 2018 Wyoming Arts Council Poetry Fellowship and has been published most recently in *Zetetic, Clerestory,* and *The Found Poetry Review*.

Matthue Roth is the author, most recently, of the novel *Rules of My Best Friend's Body* (Hevria) and the picture book *The Gobblings* (One Peace Books). By day, he's a creative writer at Google. He is a graduate of the fiction M.F.A. program at Brooklyn College and keeps a secret diary at matthue.com.

Dianne Silvestri, author of the chapbook *Necessary Sentiments,* has poems in *Main Street Rag, Earth's Daughters, The Comstock Review, Evening Street Review, The Worcester Review, The Healing Muse, The Examined Life Journal, Pulse,* and elsewhere. A Pushcart nominee, she is copy editor of *Dermatitis* and leads the Morse Poetry Group.

Mike Tuohy grew up in New Jersey during the Eisenhower years before moving to Georgia in 1965 and sopping up the Southern culture. A professional geologist working the environmental consulting rackets by day, he chronicles the preposterous through short stories and a novel-in-progress by night. Twenty of his stories have been published.

Barbara Waterman-Peters has award-winning works in museum, corporate, and private collections, and is represented by several galleries. She has shown regionally, nationally, and internationally in over 275 solo, invitational, and juried exhibitions. Waterman-Peters taught at Washburn and Kansas State universities as well as at Lassen Community College in California. She has received a Certificate of Recognition for Outstanding Achievement from the State of Kansas and the Monroe Award from the Washburn University Alumni Association.

R.S. Wynn lives in Maine on four acres that have become a de facto wild turkey preserve. She is a recent graduate of the M.F.A. in Writing program at Vermont College of Fine Arts.

Ian Andrew Young began studying art seriously in 2004, under the guidance of his father, fine art master Michael Young. He sells original paintings though galleries, art dealers, and over the internet, both locally and internationally. He has works hanging in public and private collections around the world, including Ecuador, Singapore, Russia, Australia, and the United Kingdom.

Michael Young's interest in art began as a child observing his father draw and paint in their Lansing, Kansas home. At 17 he enrolled in a two-year commercial art program in Salina. After graduation he found employment doing architectural illustration in Kansas City. He also took portrait lessons. In 1978 he moved to New York City, where he studied at the Art Students League and Salmagundi Club and took private lessons with Bill Weltman, a world-famous anatomy instructor.

www.ingramcontent.com/pod-product-compliance
Lightning Source LLC
Chambersburg PA
CBHW061107100726
47911CB00012B/430